Voiceover Narration

Voiceover Narration

Creating Performances
from the Inside Out

Dian Perry

methuen | drama

LONDON • NEW YORK • OXFORD • NEW DELHI • SYDNEY

METHUEN DRAMA
Bloomsbury Publishing Plc
50 Bedford Square, London, WC1B 3DP, UK
1385 Broadway, New York, NY 10018, USA
29 Earlsfort Terrace, Dublin 2, Ireland

BLOOMSBURY, METHUEN DRAMA and the Methuen Drama logo are
trademarks of Bloomsbury Publishing Plc

First published in Great Britain 2021

Cover design: Charlotte Daniels
Cover images © Nattspol Sritongcom / Anatolii Riabokon / Alamy

A catalogue record for this book is available from the British Library.

A catalog record for this book is available from the Library of Congress.

ISBN: HB: 978-1-3501-5851-1
PB: 978-1-3501-5850-4
ePDF: 978-1-3501-5852-8
eBook: 978-1-3501-5853-5

Typeset by Deanta Global Publishing Services, Chennai, India

To find out more about our authors and books visit www.bloomsbury.com
and sign up for our newsletters.

*For my Mom and Dad, who showed me
the power of kindness and the joy of creativity.*

Contents

Preface

For most of my adult life, I've worked as a communicator in one form or another: actor, singer, sketch and stand-up comedian, voice actor, coach, teacher, and writer. Through all of these different experiences, I've learned one immutable truth:

Connection is everything.

As performers, we can belt out show tunes, craft hilarious stand-up routines, or narrate hours of e-learning material, but if we fail to truly connect with our audience, then what's the point?

Years ago, I began to notice a disconnected quality within some narration reads. I came across many a corporate video where the narrator's voice sounded pleasant enough and the delivery seemed to be well executed, but the overall message felt hollow—it just didn't reach me as a listener. I sensed that some documentary narrators were more focused on what they *sounded* like than on sharing information with the viewer, and I saw many instructional videos where the narration simply didn't work with the visuals and music. I wanted to understand how and why performances like these missed the mark.

I began closely observing my own narration reads (internally as well as the recordings) and those of the students I was working with. It quickly became clear that there is an inextricable link between the quality of a voiceover performance and the internal workings of the performer. I'm not referring to mood or general health (though these can certainly have an effect) but rather the narrator's *investment* in the read—intellectually, physically, and emotionally. I looked at what kind of mental chatter students were contending with, where their focus was (or wasn't) being placed, and how impatience, perfectionism, and other personal tendencies were affecting their reads.

The puzzle pieces slowly came together as I began to fold these ideas and techniques into more of my teaching. The results were incredible. I witnessed astonishing improvements in students' performances, often within minutes. Once they understood and managed what was going on *inside*, everything *outside* changed.

I knew I had to write about this "psychology of narration" that I had stumbled upon and explore some interesting questions about what goes on *within* a great narrator to make them great: What happens in their mind, body, and voice, and how do they juggle it all? How do they infuse a read with authority, empathy, or drama? How do they prepare, stay focused, and manage nervous energy? In this book, you will find the answers to these questions and more, compiled from many years of observation, practice, and rooting around in the psyches of voice actors.

I must warn you, though—this is a different breed of voiceover book. You won't find tips on how a snazzy website or well-placed social media post might bring you clients, nor will you discover how to secure a voice agent or set up a home studio. There are plenty of blogs, webinars, articles, podcasts, and books which can help you in those areas. What you *will* find is a bird's-eye view of the professional narrator's mental, physical, emotional, and vocal machinery, and how you can use this knowledge to improve your skills and connect more deeply with your listener.

I am so excited to explore the fascinating inner landscape of voiceover narration with you. It is my sincere wish that, by the time you've finished this book, you'll feel ready to apply its wisdom and start creating your own outstanding performances—from the inside out.

Dian Perry
London, 2020

Acknowledgments

It is said that there is no creative endeavor quite like writing your first book and I've certainly found that to be true. I'm just really glad that I didn't have to do it alone.

I am incredibly grateful to the amazing team at Methuen Drama and I could not have asked for kinder people to work with. Special thanks go to Anna Brewer for championing my vision of a different kind of voiceover book and to Meredith Benson for answering dozens of emails with lightning speed and a welcome compassion for a new author learning the ropes.

To Charlotte Daniels—thank you for wading through my deck of rough ideas and creating a cover more stunning than I could have imagined or hoped for. Thanks as well to Robin Johnson for the wonderful graphics.

Deep love and appreciation goes to my incredible Dad—pilot, flight instructor, former air traffic controller, tech-writer, and volunteer. Thank you for your generous contributions and support. You continue to amaze and inspire me.

Thanks to my readers and advisers (your collective input was more valuable than you know): Ana Clements, Gigi Burgdorf, Leisa Fisicaro, Neil Fitzgerald, Suzanne Levy, Philippa Lubbock, Missie Biellie-Dee Luewis, Charles Nove, Joel O'Connor, Joy Swenson, Esther Wane, and Shak Yousaf. Special thanks to Ana Clements for her unique insights on audiobook narration and to Joy Swenson—thank you for all your encouragement and advice. You are a wordsmith and your suggestions were priceless.

Heartfelt thanks to my friend, teacher, and Life Alignment practitioner, Philippa Lubbock, who continually reminds me that each of us has a unique voice which needs to be heard. Thank you for teaching me that humor (among other things) must come "from the ground up."

Thanks go as well to Excellent Talent for two decades of narration opportunities, Rachael Naylor for bringing me onto the global stage as a voiceover teacher (I will always be grateful), and Yvonne Morley for generously allowing me to share a concise version of her vocal warm-up.

To my mentor, colleague, and dear friend, Charles Nove—I'm quite certain I wouldn't be where I am today without your encouragement and wise counsel. Thank you for taking me under your wing all those years ago in the art gallery basement studio.

To Bruce—my partner, helper, and quarantine companion—I don't know where I would have been without your grounded and loving support. I was drawn to write this book during very interesting times and simply could not have done it without you by my side. Thank you, my love.

And finally, so much gratitude goes to my students, especially those who graciously agreed to have their stories told. I have learned and continue to learn so much from you all. Thank you for allowing me access to your inner worlds and for helping me to uncover new pieces of the puzzle. Together, we are mapping out the secret corners of how we communicate and perform.

About the Author

Dian Perry is a US voice actor, teacher, and voiceover coach based in the UK.

Her work has been heard on narration projects, television and radio, in video games and soft toys, and on animation series and films worldwide. And if you own an older Honda in the US, chances are she will be the one telling you where to turn.

As a teacher, Dian has facilitated voiceover courses and workshops throughout London, the UK, and online to participants across the globe. In Latvia, she facilitated a two-day workshop for actors and animators as part of the Riga International Film Festival. She holds a teaching qualification and coaches students online and from her voiceover studio ("The Shed").

She lives in London with her husband.

DianPerry.com
facebook.com/dian.perry
instagram.com/dianperryvo
twitter.com/voicegirl1111

Introduction

You're about to set off for your morning walk. "Here I go!" you think. "Lift leg, bend knee, move leg forward, set foot down . . ." Of course you don't—you would probably fall over. Walking (for the most part) is automatic. You decide on a few things before you get going and the rest pretty much happens instinctively. If you constantly thought about all the mechanisms which allow you to stroll down the road *while* you stroll down the road, then you could be in serious trouble. It's the same with voiceover narration. Of course there are decisions to be made, but if you make them before you begin, then you won't need to concentrate on forming each "step" as you go along.

One of the secrets to great narration is essentially losing your mind—keeping the analytical part of your brain quiet—in order to deliver your client's message with absolute clarity. When we get distracted by mental noise, the information we're working so hard to get across becomes scattered. Trying to force a voiceover performance through a minefield of thoughts such as "How am I sounding?," "Should the inflection go up or down here?," or "Where the heck should I breathe in this mile-long paragraph?" is only going to fragment the message. The poor listener will be left trying to piece it all together and make sense of it.

In order for us to truly reach our audience, we must dare to forgo the analytical mind. You've probably never heard anyone say that they had a meaningful "head-to-head" conversation with a loved one and there's a good reason for that. The most powerful communication doesn't come from there—it comes from the heart—and I don't mean this poetically. Allow me to explain with a smattering of science.

We know that both the heart and brain generate powerful electromagnetic fields because they can be measured outside the body (with an electrocardiogram [EKG/ECG] and electroencephalogram [EEG], respectively). Surprisingly, the electrical field surrounding the heart is up to sixty times stronger in amplitude than that of the brain and the magnetic field is more than one hundred times stronger.[1]

When it comes to any kind of communication, the heart is where the action is. As speakers, when we activate this powerful center by *feeling* our way through rather than *thinking* our way through, we can transform any performance into a kind of supercharged magnet, drawing in and fully connecting with our intended audience.

At its core, voiceover narration is about authentic communication, and this is where you and I are going to begin our work together. We'll kick things off with a deep dive into the very nature of what drives human interaction, including energy, vibration, and connection. Stay with me here—this opening chapter may seem a little abstract, but I promise you that an understanding of how we relate to ourselves and each other will really help you improve your narration skills. I will also share techniques to help you narrate more intuitively and show you ways to get into (and stay in) a state of flow, rather than mentally plotting your way through a read (like thinking about every step on your walk).

Once we've explored the essence of communication, we'll look at the foundations of good narration including the mind-body-voice connection, visuals and visualizing, establishing your point of view, setting your intention, pace, formality, and knowing who you're talking to.

We'll then transfer all this knowledge and wisdom over to the practical side of voiceover narration with the five *P*s: Projects, Prep, Performance, Pitfalls, and Practice. We'll discuss the main narration subgenres and you'll be guided through the different mindsets and approaches for each. I'll show you some proven techniques for preparing and performing narration text and share some of the more common stumbling blocks (along with a few cautionary tales). You'll then have ample opportunity to practice with a wide variety of scripts and I'll provide a few notes on each to help you through (recordings of these scripts and other resources are available at: www.DianPerry.com/bookresources). By the way, the terms "script," "copy," and "text" will be used interchangeably throughout this book.

Following all of that, we'll explore what happens when you're on the job: what to expect in the studio, from the client, from yourself (if you're working alone), and what everyone else expects of you in the booth. We'll finish off with a few words of wisdom and some final thoughts.

I hope that the principles and techniques presented in this book will encourage a new vocabulary and a fresh approach to voiceover narration. As narrators and speakers in general, we have the unique privilege of conveying a message, telling a story, or imparting knowledge through the spoken word. I believe we can find our way back to doing this from a focused and authentic place, in order to have a greater impact on our listeners. Let's go for that morning walk (and enjoy the view) without tripping over our own thoughts.

1 The Essence of Communication

We humans have long used language to communicate. Whether you subscribe to the theory that it all began with Adam and Eve conspiring in the garden, or cave dwellers telling stories around the campfire, we can all agree that we've been talking to each other for a very, very long time. Language helps us to convey information, express ideas, and share feelings. In many ways, we'd be lost without it, but it does have limitations.

Imagine that every avenue of human communication was bundled into a length of fiber-optic cable. If you could slice this cord open and have a look inside, you'd see that language is only one glass strand among many. Spoken words are only one facet of how we relate to each other. We express ourselves through our eyes, tone of voice, body language, facial expressions, gestures, and (whether we choose to or not) our *energy*.

We are constantly broadcasting (and receiving) vibrational data via the body's energy gateways. Information about our inner states, thoughts, and emotions is contained within the electromagnetic fields which emanate from and surround us.[1] Unfortunately, since the time of the cave dwellers, our lives have become much more complex and we seem to have forgotten about our innate ability to influence (and tune into) these vibrations.

Over many centuries, we have trained ourselves to focus and rely more on the words we speak and hear than on the energy, intention, and emotion behind them. We have this wonderfully intricate conduit at our disposal, through which we can transmit, receive, and connect, but most of the time we limit ourselves to using a mere fraction of it. It's a bit like choosing to use a carrier pigeon instead of a cell phone.

Making the best use of our "conduit" enhances all forms of communication—from personal and business relationships to our work as speakers, voice actors, and narrators. But before we get into the actual machinery of voiceover narration, we need to recognize the underlying currents which power it: energy, intention, emotion, connection, and flow.

Together, we're going to explore these hidden depths of human communication and discover why they are so essential to a spoken word performance. Let's peer into that fiber-optic cable, look beyond the strand of language for a moment, and see what magic we can find.

Energy and Vibration

You and I are living in a giant ocean of energy. Everything we can see, touch, smell, hear, taste, or experience is part of what Einstein called "the ether" (also referred to as "the field," "the unified field," or "the superstring field") and most of the time, we aren't even aware of it.[2] We're a bit like fish, who don't know they're living in water. They swim around, feeding and breeding, without ever being conscious of what surrounds them or realizing the important role it plays in their existence. But their lack of awareness doesn't change the truth of the matter.

It's the same with the energy we're living in. We may go about living our lives mostly oblivious to it, but it still exists, and whatever happens in this immense sea of energy has an effect on everything else. Of course, we're made of the same stuff, so it makes perfect sense that we are affected by and can influence this field.

Whenever we send out waves of energy—whether in the form of thought, emotion, intention, or voice—we alter the environment we're all swimming in. It doesn't matter if we're conscious of it or not, we are constantly "feeding the field" with new vibrations every second of every day, affecting everything and everyone existing within it.[3] We cannot have a "no-energy zone" in our world any more than we can have a "no-peeing zone" in our swimming pool—it's all intermingled. This concept becomes very relevant when we start managing the quality of the vocal vibrations we send out as speakers.

Energy Speaks Louder than Words

I was a sensitive kid and have always picked up on the atmospheres in a room and the moods of those around me. I recognized early on that the *words* people spoke and the *energy* they sent out didn't always match. For example, whenever I felt that my mother was upset and I asked her about it, I would often get a conflicting response—her words assured me she was fine, but her voice and energy told a different story.

While I was growing up, I noticed many other instances in my family when people said one thing while actually meaning another. Sarcasm is a great way to achieve this, and it was a staple in our house. Humor was also part of our daily life, which was wonderful, but it could sometimes be used as a cover when one of us was feeling anything but funny. While at times confusing, these childhood experiences shaped who I have become and I'm grateful. They provided a glimpse into what lies beneath the surface layer of words. I didn't know it at the time, but this was the beginning of my life-long fascination with the energies of communication.

Energy, when charged with refined intention and emotion, is the secret ingredient in authentic communication. Without it, the spoken word (whether in daily life or performance) lacks depth and meaning. Words are merely a mechanism of expression, not expression itself. To put it another way: language is just the transport vehicle, while energy, intention, and emotion are the precious cargo. Verbal communication is essentially the transfer of vibrating energy using the processes of speech and, as you will discover throughout this book, we have the power (and responsibility) as narrators and storytellers to influence the quality of this energy.

Vibration

Nikola Tesla is famously quoted as saying that "If you want to find the secrets of the universe, think in terms of energy, frequency, and vibration."[4] This was a profound statement, especially for the 1800s, and one that has intrigued me for many years. If you've read anything about quantum physics, you will understand (at least theoretically) that everything in the perceivable universe is vibrating energy. Objects may *appear* solid but when we zoom right in, there's nothing physical there. Everything from the atoms in the chair you're sitting on to the pages of the book you're holding is essentially just wobbling energy.[5]

So how do we reconcile this with our everyday experience? It helps to remember that everything is spinning. Imagine you're driving down a country road and a tornado suddenly crosses your path. You stop the car to consider your options. You know instinctively that trying to plow through that spinning vortex would be like trying to drive through a brick wall, even though you know full well that it's mostly made of air.

Thankfully, you and I are going to be working with aspects of energy and vibration which are much easier for us mortals to grasp.

Sound and Voice

It's no great revelation to tell you that sound is vibration. We understand this very well and experience it every day. Put simply, sound is air in motion. Sound waves travel through the air (or another medium) and cause our eardrums to vibrate. These vibrations move a series of very small bones in the middle ear which then transfer the sound energy to the cochlea of the inner ear. The resulting nerve signals are then interpreted by our brains.[6] It will also be no surprise that the human voice (being sound) is vibration as well. Merriam-Webster defines *voice* as the "expiration of air with the vocal cords drawn close so as to vibrate audibly."[7]

Sound is a powerful force in our lives. Apart from catapulting us through time (who among us hasn't relived a moment when a certain song is played?), it can have a profound effect on our emotions. In fact, our brains are actually wired for it. In an article for *The Hearing Journal*, Dr. Nina Kraus, professor of auditory neuroscience at Northwestern University, wrote:

> *Hearing is coupled with feeling: In the brain, the auditory and emotional systems are interconnected by feedforward and feedback pathways, and reward-related neurotransmitters such as dopamine are expressed in the auditory centers of the brain.*[8]

As speakers and narrators, we have an enormous capacity to reach our listeners at the very deepest levels of human connection.

Emotion

Emotion also consists of vibrating energy. You only have to sit next to an angry person on the bus to know for yourself that this is true. We have the ability to sense the emotional states (vibrations) of others, even when they're not consciously or verbally expressing them. These vibrations can affect our own emotional state and even our physiology.

Most of us have, at one time or another, had an emotional reaction to an actor's performance, whether from the stage, in a film, or via the spoken word. And we've probably all experienced goose bumps in response to a beautiful piece of music or singing. When a skilled actor or singer transmits authentic emotion within a performance, we receive so much more than just story, character, and delivered lines—we are affected on a visceral level.

But what about those performances when we are expected to be emotionally moved but it doesn't happen? An actor could be doing all the "right" things physically and vocally, but if they aren't really connected to the scene or text, the performance will feel shallow. In contrast, when a performer is fully invested and *feels* what they are doing and saying, then we as the audience feel it too, and our engagement is deepened. To help illustrate this, I'll share something from my own experience.

Many years ago, I was in a London studio narrating a corporate film for a big company event. It was a call-to-action piece intended to motivate a group of global managers. The visuals were stunning and the music was a powerful orchestration worthy of John Williams himself. While I was narrating, I was completely immersed in what I was saying and experienced strong physical and emotional sensations. I had chills up and down my spine, misty eyes, and a very strong sense of pride. After the recording, I joined the others in the control room to listen to the playback and everyone else reported similar reactions.

It wasn't until years later that I put the pieces together and I know in my bones that this is true: Whatever energies we generate within are transmitted through the vocal vibrations of speech and into the ears of the listener:

What we feel, our audience feels.

This realization changed the way I would approach every single voiceover project. If I wanted to evoke a visceral reaction in the listener, I was going to have to put my whole self (energy and all) into every read, every time. In order to fully connect with my audience, I would need to do so much more than just read the words and make them sound pretty.

Resonance and Connection

The term *resonate* is used a lot these days. It has become a real buzzword, as in "That idea really resonates with me" or "I really resonated with what that person said." But what does it actually mean? Merriam-Webster defines *resonate* as: "to relate harmoniously; strike a chord."[9] In other words—to make a connection.

Whenever we speak to anyone in any capacity, our primary goal is always to connect with them on some level. We want our audience to absorb, understand, and respond to what we've said. We may wish to evoke a certain emotion, encourage an individual or group to take a particular action, learn something new, or simply relax and allow themselves to be entertained. Whatever our specific intention as speakers, we always hope that our message resonates with the listener and that they are "in tune" with whatever we're communicating.

The Sympathetic Tuning Fork

Picture a pair of identical tuning forks standing side by side, which are both tuned to the exact same frequency. Forks tuned to an "A," for example, are said to have a frequency of 440 Hertz (Hz) as this musical note has been set to vibrate at a rate of 440 cycles per second.[10] When just one of our pair of forks is struck, the other vibrates "in sympathy" and will continue to do so even after the first one has been silenced. This occurs because the second fork (which has not been struck) has been affected by the vibrating air molecules around the first, producing a "sympathetic resonant vibration."[11]

When a person resonates with something, whether it's the presence of another individual, a fresh new concept, or a spoken word performance, what's occurring is an alignment of frequency. The listener has effectively become the second tuning fork, resonating with the vibrations of the source. To put it simply—they're on the same wavelength.

As narrators, storytellers, and speakers, we take on the role of the first tuning fork, sending out a message (vocal vibrations) in the hope that our listeners will resonate and vibrate in sympathy with us. Of course, we can (and often do) resort to manipulating our vocal delivery in an effort to *force* a connection with the audience, but communication is much more powerful when it occurs organically—when our intention is clear and our own "fork" is precisely tuned. Let me illustrate this with a personal story.

It was a gorgeous, sunny spring day and I was walking down the street while listening to *Mandolin Rain* by Bruce Hornsby and the Range at full volume through my earphones. I was feeling fantastic as I bounced along in the sunshine. I noticed a tall, thin man walking toward me dressed in a tattered raincoat and beanie hat. As we were about to pass each other, he held up his hand as if to give me a high five. Before my critical faculties could kick in, I smiled at him, slapped his hand, and we each went on our way. Seconds later, I was stunned by what had just happened. It was well outside my usual behavior to high-five a total stranger in the street, but my blissful state had rendered me completely open to human connection, without judgment. I thought about that encounter many times, and eventually reached a level of understanding about how it came to be.

Positive emotions such as gratitude, joy, kindness, and love, create much higher vibrations in the body and I was certainly firing on all cylinders that morning.[12] Because I was fully connected *inside*, I was able to easily connect *outside*. This realization led me to a mind-bending "chicken and egg" question: did the quality of my energy make me more receptive to an event that was going to take place anyway, or did the event take place *because* of the quality of my energy? I may never be able to answer that question, but I do know this: the more harmonious we are as individuals, the stronger our capacity for authentic communication, connection, and that most desirable of performance states—flow.

Flow and Coherence

Flow

Merriam-Webster defines *flow* as "a smooth uninterrupted movement or progress."[13] In psychology terms, however, the concept of flow refers to the positive mental state when we are so completely immersed and absorbed in a task, that the rest of the world seems to fade away and all sense of time is lost. Positive psychologist Mihaly Csikszentmihalyi, who began his study of flow and the creative process back in the 1960s, describes it this way:

> Being completely involved in an activity for its own sake. The ego falls away. Time flies. Every action, movement, and thought follows inevitably from the previous one, like playing jazz. Your whole being is involved, and you're using your skills to the utmost.[14]

Personally, I experience creative flow as a sort of intensely focused awareness, where intuition, communication, and creativity seem effortless and otherworldly. Time warps around me and hours seem to pass in the blink of an eye. I forget to eat and hardly notice when day turns into night. You may recognize this as "being in the zone" and for artists, performers, speakers, and storytellers alike, it is pure heaven.

Imagine yourself settling into the voice booth to narrate an audiobook or stepping up to the lectern to deliver a speech. Any extraneous thoughts quickly fade away, your focus narrows to the task at hand, and you almost feel as though you've stepped into an alternate reality. You cannot say precisely how it's happening, but you are effortlessly transforming the text on the page into a coherent and connected performance. The words seem to go from your eyes to your body and voice with only a whisper of input from your mind. Even when you make a mistake, you are not distracted; you simply stop for a split second, pick up the last line, and continue as if nothing ever happened. This is what it feels like to be in full flow as a speaker—to transcend the analytical mind and reach a place of pure expression.

Coherence

When we have this most welcome experience of being fully present and in a state of flow, it's an indication that our internal systems are fully aligned and coherent. Dr. Rollin McCraty, author and director of research at the HeartMath Institute, defines coherence as: "Clarity of thought, speech and emotional composure."[15] Tell me that doesn't sound like the perfect recipe for a great performance.

There are three primary systems which, when balanced and working as a whole (coherently), can completely transform your spoken word performances: Mind–Body–Voice, Heart–Brain, and The 7 Wavelengths of Communication.

Mind–Body–Voice

This trio forms the foundational circuit for verbal communication. Successfully managing this system and keeping the elements in balance is vital to any type of spoken word performance. We're going to cover it in much greater detail in the next chapter, when we talk about the foundations of narration.

Heart–Brain

As we're discovering, the most authentic and connected performances are instinctive and intuitive. But how do we get into this state, where we operate more from intuition than mental analysis? One way is to encourage the heart and brain to work together in harmony. Author and speaker Gregg Braden summarizes this concept beautifully: "When we harmonize our heart and our brain, what we're doing is opening a hotline to the subconscious."[16]

As you probably know, the heart and brain are in constant communication, but what may be surprising is that the heart actually does most of the talking. In fact, the heart sends more information to the brain than vice versa at a ratio of 90:1.[17] Also, the heart contains around 40,000 specialist cells that can sense, feel, learn, and remember. These "sensory neurites" have collectively been termed "the little brain in the heart."[18] The heart plays a much more important role in our lives than just pumping blood around the body. But what does all this have to do with spoken word performance?

If we want to truly reach our listener, we have got to retrain ourselves to speak more from the heart than the brain. And we cannot access our heart's intelligence through plotting, planning, vocal manipulation, or any other function of the analytical mind. The only way in is to step into the *feeling* of what we are saying, which creates heart-brain harmony and coherence. In Chapter 4, I'll show you how you can tangibly shift your energy from the head to the heart.

The 7 Wavelengths of Communication

At the beginning of this chapter, the aspects of human communication were likened to glass strands within a fiber-optic cable. We're now going to look at seven of these strands, which I refer to collectively as "The 7 Wavelengths of Communication." These are key components of how we relate to one another and when they work together in a balanced way, the quality of any communication is vastly improved. In Chapter 5, we'll talk more about folding them into a cohesive spoken word performance. But for now, let's find out what they are, beginning with a little visualization.

Imagine you're having lunch with a dear friend. You're immersed in deep conversation and expressing your innermost thoughts and feelings. You are each sensing a strong connection to the other and it's as if the outside world has disappeared. Now visualize that concentrated energetic link as a full-spectrum beam of light (like a rainbow) where each color represents a different layer—or wavelength—within your exchange:

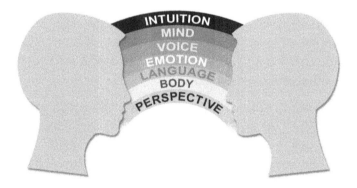

Figure 1 The 7 Wavelengths of Communication.

Whenever we engage in any type of spoken communication, whether it's that intimate conversation with our friend, an argument with our partner, or an e-learning narration, these seven wavelengths will be operating. Let's look at each one more closely, starting with the base and moving upward.

Perspective
Within any form of verbal exchange, every individual has their own point of view. For example, each person may be in favor of

or against something, curious about a topic, or speaking from a place of authority or conviction.

In everyday life, we don't always know our listener's perspective and thus we must sense and react as we go along. But in voiceover, we have the luxury of knowing this information in advance. After all, most projects are carefully crafted to reach a specific group of people who share a particular point of view.

For every type of narration project, you'll need to know where both you (as the narrator) and your audience stand.

Body
Communication is a full-body activity. We talk with our hands, raise our eyebrows, involuntarily mime along with what we're saying, furrow our brows, and experience emotional energies coursing through our bodies. In narration (as with any genre of voiceover) you cannot omit body involvement simply because the voice is the only part of the performance to ultimately be captured. We'll talk about the power of gesturing and physicality in Chapter 5, and look at why they are so important in getting your message across.

Language
There is no question that we're able to communicate without words. Facial expressions, body language, and energy can all convey thoughts, ideas, and emotions. Of course for our purposes as narrators, language is a key component and absolutely essential. Text is the framework on which our message is carefully crafted in order to reach our intended listener. However, it's important to remember that language is just the courier—it's up to the speaker to provide the energetic cargo.

Emotion
We don't always acknowledge emotion when we're speaking, but as we've discovered, its energy signature is usually present in the background. Extreme states such as exuberance or

outrage will be obvious, but there are many subtle emotions we may project subconsciously such as pride, confidence, and hope. Feeling your way into what you're saying is an important layer in the communication spectrum.

Voice

The human voice is a wondrous thing and its power cannot be overstated. When it works in harmony with the other wavelengths, it can inform, comfort, entice, convince, energize, inspire, tickle, and more. We can send it on its way, loaded only with dry words and manipulated vocal tones, or we can choose to fully infuse it with intention, emotion, and life force.

Surprisingly, voice is not the primary focus in a spoken word performance. Earlier in the chapter, I wrote "Language is just the transport vehicle, while energy, intention, and emotion are the precious cargo." At the risk of mangling this metaphor beyond all recognition—voice is the fuel—it turbo-charges language in order to deliver the refined energies of a communication.

Intuition

Intuition is tricky to pin down, but it's such an important part of what we do as voice actors, storytellers, and speakers. Collins dictionary defines *intuition* as "knowledge or belief obtained neither by reason nor by perception."[19] Many people (myself included) think of intuition as a form of higher consciousness or the "Higher Self," while others might prefer to think of it as "the little voice in your head." However you choose to view it, intuition is a link to something greater than ourselves and developing our ability to tap into it (or *allow* it, to be more precise) is a game changer.

But before you can access and rely on this guidance, you have to clear a path for it. First, you need to get calm. Intuition cannot reach you through a tangle of nerves and a mind full of scrambled thoughts. Second (and this is the big one) you need to *trust* that if you're aligned and present, your intuition will engage and your speech will naturally flow.

Mind

It might seem obvious to say that we have to think in order to communicate, but the *way* in which we use our minds (or don't) is a really important factor. We've all had the experience of talking to someone and witnessing their "listening light" fade out and their "thinking light" flicker on. At that point, they have switched off from hearing what *we* have to say and are busy constructing in their heads what *they* have to say.

This is what the mind does—it pushes its way to the front and tries to drive a conversation or performance. We must gently "re-mind" it that it's not the only wavelength in town and needs to play nice with the others.

In the next chapter, we'll talk about the mind-body-voice connection, and in Chapters 5 and 6, how the mind should and shouldn't behave while we're performing.

Obviously, I don't advise that you think about these seven wavelengths while you're in the midst of a conversation or narration read (I believe I've previously covered why this muddies the waters). Rather, use them as a reference guide for a verbal exchange or performance and practice becoming aware of any imbalances.

Summary

This opening chapter is probably not what you expected to find in a book about voiceover narration. But as I mentioned in the Introduction, having a greater understanding of how we relate to ourselves and each other, really does improve narration performances. I have witnessed it time and time again with students and have experienced it in my own work as well.

In this chapter, we've explored human communication and connection at their most fundamental levels: energy, intention, and emotion. When we approach our narration performances from this perspective, our reads come alive and our listeners are hooked. Energy really does speak louder than words.

As narrators, storytellers, and speakers in general, the question we should ask ourselves is not "How can I manipulate my voice to sound like I imagine it should?" but rather "How can I manage the energy, intention, and emotion which will then inform and influence the sound of my voice?" If we want a visceral reaction from our audience, we need to put our entire selves (energy and all) into every read, every time.

2 **The Foundations of Narration**

Now that we've explored the driving forces of human communication and connection, we can move on to the foundations which support a great narration read. In the Introduction, the analogy of going for a walk was used to illustrate that narration is mostly instinctive, once you've decided on a few things. In this chapter, we're going to focus on what these decisions are, how to go about making them, and the positive impact this will all have on your performances.

But before we launch into this fresh approach to voiceover narration, let me say a little about current trends as I see them.

Top Down

Many voice actors prepare for narration using what I call the "top down" method (as it reminds me of building a house by starting with the roof) and I worked this way myself for a very long time. The preparation usually begins with a mental analysis about which words or phrases to emphasize, where to pause, change inflection, take a breath, and so on. The choices are then noted within the text in order to create a kind of road map for the read. But there's a paradox with this strategy—it attempts to create depth within a performance by making adjustments at the surface level.

Emphases, pauses, and inflection are certainly necessary in a spoken word performance, but prescribing each and every one of them is not. These aspects of speech will usually occur naturally once the proper foundations have been put in place. Plotting every utterance and then trying to follow that "map" during a read will keep you firmly rooted in the analytical mind and out of the flow.

Although I worked this way for many years, it now reminds me of those dance step diagrams which were popular in the 1950s. We may be able to mechanically follow the numbered footprints, but that doesn't mean we've mastered the foxtrot. I believe a great many voice actors have become adept at (and much too reliant upon) using a vocal version of the dance diagram. We have learned by rote the "steps" of how to manipulate our voices and manufacture a decent delivery, but much of the time, we're not really "dancing."

Outside In

On the other side of the glass, many producers and directors tend to work "from the outside in." They usually have a clear idea of what they want the final performance to sound like, but aren't always aware of what needs to happen in the narrator's mind, body, and voice in order to achieve it. As a result, direction is often focused on aspects of the finished vocal delivery (inflection, pitch, pauses, and so on) rather than the fundamentals on which they were built. If directors were to address the foundational elements when working with voice actors, they would draw out much better performances. Let me give you an example.

It's quite common during a session for voice actors to receive direction such as "make the inflection go up on the company name" or "pause for two seconds after that line." This guidance may encourage a slightly different sounding read, but unless the underlying rationale is understood by the narrator, any changes to the performance are likely to be superficial—vocal manipulation versus authentic communication. If, on the other hand, the director suggests something like "this is where pride in the company needs to shine through" or "we need to give the listener more time to let that information sink in," then the performance can be adjusted at its most basic level, thus preserving its integrity:

Change the foundations and the entire "house" shifts.

So, what are these foundations which are so essential to producing great narration reads? What kind of solid base do we need to build in order to free ourselves as speakers to clearly express our clients' messages and stories? Let's start off with the most crucial bit of groundwork—getting your mind, body, and voice to work together as a team.

The Mind-Body-Voice Connection

As individual speakers, voice actors, and narrators, we are always working with a crew of three—a sort of "holy trinity" of performance—mind, body, and voice (MBV). When this trio works as one, our reads flow very nicely; when their paths diverge, not so much. Luckily, we're equipped with the innate ability to sense when our components are working well together and when they are not.

Try this exercise: slump down in a chair and let all the energy drain out of your body. Keep still and exclaim "I am alive and I feel fantastic!" How did you do? Chances are there was an inner conflict between the words you said and how you felt saying them. Collapsed in your chair, your body was in quite a low state of vibration while your mind and voice were trying to generate something with a very high vibration. I refer to this uncomfortable experience as "disconnect." If your MBV are not on the same page, you're going to feel that pinch of disconnection and your message will have a tough time getting through.

Let's do another: stand up straight and strong with your feet shoulder width apart, chin up in the air, and hands on your hips. Now quietly whisper "I am a superhero, and I am here to save the world!" Did you feel the discord between your body language, voice, and the information you were trying to get across? Perhaps you instinctively tried to pull it all together into something that made sense and felt true? This is a really good impulse to cultivate and will help to keep your MBV working as one. When I tried this exercise, I imagined I was standing in front of a mirror, having donned my superhero outfit for the first time; I was smiling at the reflection and tentatively trying out a catch phrase.

It's an odd sensation when the MBV are out of sync. Learn to recognize this feeling (however it manifests for you) and trust it, because it's going to be a useful early warning signal when your performance goes off track.

Think of MBV as a circular system, where any one of the three elements can be used as an entry point, depending on your learning style. For example, if you tend to be cerebral, start there and then add physicality and voice; if you are naturally more body-focused, begin with gesturing and then let the voice and mind join in; if you're aural (like me) get your voice going and then allow the mind and body to follow. It doesn't matter where you start, so long as the trio ultimately works together as one system and in balance. Let's get to know the members of your team.

Mind

In the Introduction, I wrote "In order for us to truly reach our audience, we must dare to forgo the analytical mind." Let me expand on that. The goal is not to stop using your mind altogether, just to keep the critical part in check so it doesn't interfere with your performance. So, where is this meddling critic and how can we control it? I'll answer both parts of that question, but first we need to know a little about how our brains are wired.

Right and Left Brain

I have to admit that I knew relatively little about brain anatomy before a friend recommended Dr. Jill Bolte Taylor's incredible 2008 TED Talk, "My Stroke of Insight." Using an actual human organ, Dr. Bolte Taylor teaches us that our brains are divided into two distinct hemispheres and that the right and left halves are mostly independent, apart from a thick bridge of fibers called the corpus callosum.[1]

The right brain sees everything in pictures. It's focused on the present moment and learns kinesthetically (through movement). This is also the part of the brain which connects our consciousness to the energy all around us. The left brain thinks in language rather than pictures. It's concerned with logic; it categorizes, is methodical, and sees the world as "I" and "other." This is where our inner critic lives and it's also where our language and numbers reside.

In her gripping eighteen-minute presentation, Dr. Bolte Taylor shares her extraordinary experience of having a stroke, while witnessing it from her unique perspective as a brain scientist. She suffered a massive hemorrhage in her left hemisphere which rendered her unable to speak, recognize numbers, or recall any of her life. It took eight years, but she made a full recovery to astonish the world with her story. I watched this inspiring talk many times, and it must have planted a seed.

Years later, I was teaching a class on voice acting for animation and had a revelation about the different hemispheres of the brain and the roles they play in performance. Working with a group of students, I was using a slightly amended version of Pat Fraley's Two-column Exercise for character creation.[2] The game is based on two numbered lists—one containing character descriptors (silly, crazy, sarcastic) and the other, a list of character types (farmer, clown, professor). A student chooses two numbers between one and twenty-one and the next person in the circle has to come up with a character based on that combination. After a short improvised performance, they choose two numbers for the next person, and so on.

After using this exercise many times, I began to notice something very peculiar. Sometimes, when a student finished improvising a character, they would forget about choosing two numbers for the next person and would simply stand there, looking bemused. When I reminded them, they would invariably shake their head as if being awakened from a daydream and then announce their numbers. What was going on here? After a while, a pattern emerged. It appeared that the deeper a student went into character, the more likely it was that they would forget the number part of the exercise.

Eventually, I connected these observations with what I had come to understand about the right and left hemispheres of the brain; I developed a working theory and kept it in mind during future classes. Time and again, I witnessed the same thing—the students who were fully immersed in their characters experienced a delay before being able to select their random numbers. Was it possible that the most connected performances were rooted in the right brain? If a student was really flying with their improv and completely present in the performance, I just knew they would need a couple of seconds to switch hemispheres to get their numbers. I swear, sometimes I could almost hear a "clunk"!

As this particular exercise was always improvised, I was curious to see if the theory held with script-based performances. I started applying it to narration workshops and the results were intriguing. While performances using written material will naturally engage more of the left brain (where the language center is located) those students who used visualization, movement, or were more emotionally invested (all of which are primarily right brain functions) gave much stronger reads and connected more fully with the audience.

The right and left brains are very different characters. One side is like a child who wants to go outside, run around, play in the mud and regard everything with curiosity and wide-eyed wonder. The other is more like an overprotective parent who wants to schedule, control, and count everything. It warns of stranger danger, getting too dirty, and is always telling you to pay attention and stop daydreaming. You've probably worked out that the "child" is your right brain and the "parent" is your left. Obviously, we cannot control the hemispheres of our brain the way we might control our eyebrows, but we can learn to sense where a performance is coming from and make any necessary corrections.

We've all seen acting performances which seemed stilted, wooden, or self-conscious. While we don't have brain scans of these actors while they were working, there's a very good chance that their left hemispheres were getting in the way.

As voice actors, we need to work from the left (the adult) for script prep and decision making, and then switch to the right (the child) for the actual performance. We'll look at techniques on how to do this and talk more about the mind in performance in Chapter 5.

Body

Close your eyes and imagine yourself giving a TED Talk on a subject very close to your heart. Picture yourself relating to and connecting with your audience, basking in that delicious exchange of energy, and referring to your beautifully prepared slides on the big screen behind you. Got the picture? Now, are you standing perfectly still with your arms at your sides? Of course not—you're using your entire body to express your ideas and help the audience understand and connect to what you have to say. So why would you take body movement out of the equation when you're speaking in front of a microphone?

Obviously, when you're narrating at the mic, you won't be able to walk around or move your head too much, but you can move your hands and to some extent, your entire body. Even limited gesturing with one hand can magically enhance your read. Moving the body—even a little—sends a signal to your narration machinery that the "B" in your MBV is active and in the game. Test it out for yourself. Record a portion of text while you're completely still and then again with gestures or subtle body movement. I promise you that the performance with body involvement will have more depth and more life.

Trisha's Story

While we should always make a habit of engaging the body during a voiceover performance, sometimes a preexisting association can actually interfere with a read. There could be an unconscious link between certain body movements and a particular attitude or quality of vocal expression.

Trisha attended one of my narration workshops. We were doing a recording exercise and the microphone was situated so that the students would need to stand while narrating. From the moment Trisha stood up from her chair and started to walk toward the microphone, her entire demeanor changed. She seemed to morph into a completely different person than the one we had all just been happily chatting with. Her manner became slightly stern and once at the mic, she projected much more than what was necessary and her delivery was very formal and rigid, regardless of the text she was working with.

It turned out that Trisha was a criminal lawyer (an English barrister, to be precise). She recognized that an instinctive pattern had been ingrained in her from years of presenting cases in open court. When a barrister stands to speak, certain attitudes, behaviors, and vocal tones kick in automatically. Once we got her a chair and lowered the microphone, Trisha's reads instantly changed. Now that she's aware of the mechanisms at play, she can begin to form new associations for her narration work. With practice, she will be in complete command of her skills, regardless of whether she is sitting or standing.

Voice

As we explored in the opening chapter, voice is not the primary focal point while you're narrating, but rather the end product. The voice is infused with whatever is generated in the body-mind—energy, intentions, and emotion. Of course we may still need to mechanically change the sound of our voice for different projects and character work, but we always want that solid layer of authenticity to support it.

There may be those who believe that a beautiful voice is enough to carry them through a voiceover performance. They may argue that they really don't need to do much more than simply read aloud. Allow me to address this school of thought with a simple allegory: let's say that you own a radio station which transmits at a frequency of 100 Megahertz (MHz) but all of your listeners own radios which are tuned to 107 MHz. Your broadcast is not getting through to them, no matter what beautiful music your station may be playing.

Positioning

When preparing for narration, you must always consider your position—not whether you are sitting or standing—but rather your point of view. For example, in corporate narration, you will almost always be speaking from one of two positions: a representative of the company or an outside authority. For an audiobook, you might have the role of impartial narrator (aside from any character dialog) or you may be speaking from a character's perspective who is part of the story.

The copy will usually clue you in about your position as the speaker. For example, in a corporate script, phrases such as "we've had a record year" or "we aim to create lasting change in our world" are indications that you'll be speaking as a member of the organization. Adopting this position will naturally infuse your read with a sense of pride. You won't need to actively do anything—just recognizing that you're speaking as an insider will naturally create subtle changes in the read.

In contrast, if the text is more like "company X has developed a new product" or "they are leading the way in sustainability" then you're sure to be delivering the message as an outside authority. In this case, your read will instinctively tend to be more formal. Again, simply acknowledging this position will inform the read—you don't need to do anything else.

For audiobooks, narrating as a character who is telling the main part of the story will be very different than reading as a neutral narrator. A character will have some level of investment in the story and will have opinions about the other characters and events. For example, *The Lovely Bones* by Alice Sebold is written in first person, with the character of Susie Salmon telling the story of her own murder. The events are described from her perspective, and we understand her experiences both before and after her death. It would be impossible (and ridiculous) to approach this audiobook as an impartial narrator. The listener must believe that 14-year-old Susie is speaking to them from "her heaven" and they must care about what happened to her and what she feels and comes to understand about it.

Determining the positioning for any type of narration requires only a quick assessment, but making the choice will provide consistent depth and clarity to your reads. Let's dig a little further into the roles of both narrator and listener.

Identifying the Players

In addition to acknowledging your general position or point of view for each narration project, you must also know the answers to these three important questions:

1. Who are you?
2. Who are you talking to?
3. What do you want from the audience?

These questions are not only the cornerstones of a voiceover read (or any type of performance, for that matter) but also for conversations in general. You may not be aware of asking or answering them in your daily life because it happens automatically.

Let's look at the first two of these questions and consider this scenario: you're at a bar having a few drinks and a fun time with friends. Your phone rings and you see that it's your doctor's office calling to give you the results of a recent scan. Chances are you're going to step outside where it's quiet and completely change your demeanor to have that conversation. You have subconsciously (and very quickly) made the choice to switch from "rowdy drinking buddy" to "attentive patient" based solely on who you're talking to, and you will probably speak more clearly (despite the alcohol) and come across as much more formal.

Determining your role for a narration project can happen in a flash too, but it may take a little practice and experience for it to become an instant reflex. Until then, you'll just need to spend a little time considering it for each script.

As for the third question (What do you want from the audience?) anything you could possibly ask of them in response to your narration performance can be neatly distilled into four categories (LEAF):

1. **L**earn
2. **E**xperience
3. **A**ct
4. **F**eel

A quick assessment is really all that's needed. Once again, there is nothing specific for you to do—simply making the choice will create subtle changes in your read.

In Character

Personally, I approach every narration project as though I'm playing a character. This mindset helps me get into "performance mode" as opposed to "reading mode." Preparing to perform a character (however similar they are to me) triggers my acting muscles and puts me in a more heightened state than I would be for merely reading aloud. I suppose it's a kind of psychological trick I play on myself, but it works for me. Find what works for you and go with it.

Character work within most types of narration project is a much more subtle undertaking than that of, say, video games or animation. Most of the time, it's more about summoning a facet of yourself which fits the bill, than it is creating a fully formed character from scratch. We all have different character traits which we can draw from. For example, you might be a stern business person, loving partner, strict parent, and compassionate friend all at the same time. Choose from the various roles you play in life for your narration characters. They're sure to be believable, because they're you!

For some narration projects, however, you *will* be required to create full-blown characters. Children's audiobooks, for example, generally call for a narrator as well as several well-developed characters to bring the story to life. We'll talk more about character voice creation in Chapter 4, as well as other special requirements for audiobooks.

In summary, as outlined in the doctor's call example, we subconsciously change the way we relate to others depending on who we're talking to. The bottom line is that you always need to know who you are and who you're talking to in order to provide context and a framework for what you're about to say.

The 3 Dials

The next foundational tool is something I call "The 3 Dials." Setting these imaginary controls as part of narration prep has made a huge difference in my own voice work and a great many students have embraced it as well. Workshop participants often report that the intention dial in particular has been "a game changer" for them.

Using this technique to "dial in" your delivery before you narrate frees you up to perform more intuitively and keeps you from getting tangled up in thought during your read. Making a few simple decisions before you begin will change your performance in ways you won't even have to think about. Let's take a closer look at each one.

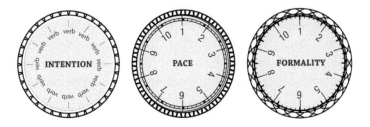

Figure 2 The 3 Dials.

Intention

It's fairly difficult to deliver a message if you don't know *why* you're delivering it. Without the energy of a specific purpose behind what you're saying, the words will have minimal impact and may even float away unnoticed, no matter how beautiful your voice sounds. You need the grounding power of intention in order to create a solid delivery which reaches—and has an effect upon—your target audience.

The intention for a narration read is a single action word—a specific verb which accurately defines what you're trying to achieve with the communication. Do you want to entice, convince, guide, seduce, or something else entirely? Setting your intention gives you a solid platform from which to speak. It anchors the message and keeps your read consistent. The more specific the intention, the more nuanced the performance.

For example, you could decide that the intention for your science-fiction audiobook is to "entertain" but this is very general and wouldn't really do much to clarify your read or distinguish it from most other novels. However, if you chose something like "mystify," this is much more specific, and your read would reflect this without you having to consciously do anything.

Once you've set your intention for a project, let it go. There is no need to hold the word in your head throughout the read or engage in mental analysis about how it's going to affect your performance—the act of declaring it is enough. It's as if the instruction goes straight into your narration machinery's operating system, which knows instinctively what to do with it. You will now be able to connect with the feeling of the message or story rather than trying to mentally control the read. In other words, your performance will be coming from the heart and not the head.

There are countless verbs you can choose from in order to set a refined intention for your narration reads and Table 1 contains

Table 1 List of Intentions

advise	enthrall	pacify
amuse	enthuse	placate
announce	entice	prepare
assist	escort	present
attract	establish	persuade
awaken	excite	prompt
beguile	exhilarate	propose
brief	explain	provoke
cajole	fascinate	reassure
captivate	galvanize	recommend
caution	guide	remind
charm	illuminate	revive
coach	incite	reward
comfort	induce	school
commend	influence	seduce
convince	inform	sell
counsel	instigate	shock
dazzle	inspire	soothe
delight	instruct	stimulate
demonstrate	intrigue	stir
denounce	introduce	suggest
describe	invigorate	teach
document	invite	tell
educate	lament	tempt
elucidate	launch	tickle
enchant	mesmerize	train
encourage	motivate	unite
endorse	move	urge
energize	mystify	update
enlighten	nominate	usher
entertain	notify	warn

quite a long list to get you started. Initially, you could choose a few which might be relevant, but try to refine it to the one that feels most right. Choosing just the right intention will focus the energy of your communication with laser-like accuracy.

Of course, if the content and tone of the project warrant it, you could have a different intention for each section of the text. This works well for audiobooks, but try to refrain from setting multiple intentions for other types of narration unless you've identified tangible gear changes within the copy.

Pace

Oftentimes, there is a narrow range of tempo we must keep within to ensure that our listeners stay with us—too slow and they might get bored; too fast and they may fall behind and become frustrated. There are four main factors which will affect the pace of a narration read:

1. Subject

In a documentary, for example, a voiceover about roller coasters is likely to be quicker-paced than one about the lifecycle of sea turtles. Another example would be language training (LT), where a project for Level 1 learners would be a great deal slower than one for Level 5.

2. Timing

If the visuals on a project are already locked in, you'll need to adjust your pace in order to read within the allotted time. Also, the script may be overwritten (or underwritten) in which case you may need to make adjustments.

3. Emotion

We tend to speak more quickly when emotions are heightened (whether it's excitement, outrage, or nervousness) and conversely, our pace naturally slows when we talk of somber things, such as poverty or loss.

Another emotional factor which informs the pace of a read is music. It would sound fairly strange to have a lightning-quick narration read over a music bed of Beethoven's "Moonlight Sonata." Always ask the producer if you can hear the chosen music or at least find out what they have in mind for the piece.

4. Project

The pace of a read will vary depending on the type of project. For those where the listener needs to consider and absorb information (such as e-learning) the read would be much slower; those which are intended to motivate or excite a workforce will generally call for a quicker-paced read.

As voice actors, we don't always have much say regarding the final pace of a read. There may be production factors or client demands which mean that a read has to be slower or faster than our instincts tell us it should be. And while our aim is to please the client, I think it's fine to speak up (albeit cautiously) if the pace of a read really doesn't feel right. This rarely comes as a surprise, as it probably won't sound right either.

Setting the pace dial from 1–10 (one being inhumanly slow and ten being ridiculously fast) isn't an exact science, but simply making a choice sends a signal about how your mind-body-voice needs to prepare. Unless you're narrating strictly to time, you won't even need to consider your choice during the read. For example, if you set your pace dial to nine, you will naturally gear up for a race. You might instinctively take an extra deep breath and your heart may start beating a little faster. Just remember that the pace has to feel right—both to the narrator and the listener—and must blend well with the other project elements.

Formality

As previously discussed, we communicate differently depending on who we're talking to. If we're at a job interview, we express ourselves very differently than if we're at Sunday brunch with a pal and a mimosa. As narrators, we have to calibrate the formality of our delivery to the listener. Are we talking to toddlers learning their first words or to oncologists about the next big cancer treatment?

Setting the formality dial for your reads (one being very laid-back and casual, and ten being more of a human-robot hybrid) can help you reach your intended audience at the appropriate level. Just know who you're talking to and the message will find its way right to them.

Visuals and Visualizing

Visuals

Vision is our dominant sense. In fact, around one-third of our brains are devoted to it, so any visuals within a narration project will naturally take center stage.[3] The voiceover then supports what's being seen and provides supplemental information to the viewer. One of our tasks as narrators is to craft a performance that blends seamlessly with any images, without overpowering them.

The visuals within a narration production could be video, animation, film, a PowerPoint presentation, a series of still photographs, or a screen capture from an app. It's always a good idea to find out what the visuals are for a project. Don't be shy about asking—this is part of what you need to know in order to do your job well. If the final images aren't available, your client should at least be able to give you an idea of what's being planned so you can craft your performance accordingly.

Some projects (such as on hold messaging and audiobooks) won't have accompanying visuals. In these cases, the narration can step up and be the star of the show, where the full responsibility of telling the story or communicating the client's message rests with you and your delivery.

Visualizing

You may recall from the previous chapter that the most connected performances seem to come from the right side of the brain, which thinks in pictures. Visualization is a very useful tool to keep you operating from this intuitive side and it also gives your reads a "three-dimensional" quality. Let me give you an example: if you've ever watched someone talk about their recent vacation, you've probably noticed that glimmer in their eye which told you that they were reliving it—picturing the scenes while they described the experience to you—which added dimension to the story and helped bring it to life.

If you're not narrating to picture, it's a good idea to find something else to visualize. If you don't, you risk slipping into a read which could upstage the visuals, once everything is mixed together. You could visualize:

1. What you're talking about.
2. An approximation of what the production images will be.
3. A scene between you and your listener.

Let's look at this last one. By visualizing yourself speaking directly to your audience, all the nuances of this imaginary communication effortlessly come forth in your read. It's almost magical. Try this exercise: find yourself a dry piece of copy to work with (such as the technical script in Chapter 7). Choose a short segment and record it with no visualization—just focus on the words and how you think they should be read. Then switch it up and record each subsequent take while visualizing yourself speaking to a variety of listeners:

1. A large crowd in an auditorium during your TED talk.
2. One person at their computer, who is learning.
3. A five-year-old child (reading them a bedtime story).
4. A group of sales managers (trying to motivate them).

If you were able to visualize the scenes clearly (or even just get a strong sense of them) chances are you'll hear the subtle differences in your recorded reads.

Here's a very specific visualization that I use whenever I narrate an e-learning project: I'm sitting at a round table with a student to my left. There is an open textbook lying on the table between us and I'm gently guiding them through the lessons. Visualizing this scene greatly improves my narration in a number of ways:

1. Keeps me out of my analytical left brain.
2. Informs the pace (e-learning is generally slower to allow time for the listener to absorb information).
3. Gives the read an intimate sense of one-to-one communication.

Making good use of the visualization tool has seen me through some complicated jobs. I once worked on a long-term narration project created for oil and gas engineers. Every Monday for nearly a year, I would travel to the studio with a three-inch stack of pages and talk about complex machinery which I knew nothing about. Even though I had no idea what any of this equipment looked like or how it operated, I visualized it as I went through the text (and used my hands a lot to help describe it) and this worked a treat. Okay, the machines in my head were more like something out of a Dr. Seuss book, but it didn't matter—I was describing *something* that I could see in my mind's eye, which brought depth and clarity to the reads.

We Are How We Speak

There really is no getting around it—how we communicate is a reflection of who we are. Of course, we can counteract any unwanted tendencies by using our acting and vocal skills, but the vibrations of who we are and how we're feeling in the moment will always seep through into our performances. Any underlying personal issues will continue to surface and contaminate our reads until we acknowledge them and learn to let them go.

Viola's Story

Viola came to see me for a coaching session. We had been working on getting her ready to record a narration demo and this was our fourth meeting. One of the trouble spots we'd been trying to resolve was a stubborn habit she'd developed of dropping into a forceful, overly melodic newsperson-style read. The "song" was nearly identical for every sentence and phrase, with the pitch going down at the end (as is so often heard in a newsreader delivery). It was such a strong association for me as a listener that after every line, I could almost hear the unspoken "and now over to Bob for the weather." I relayed this observation to Viola, who recognized the similarity, and we had a good laugh about it.

Whenever I'm listening to students' voiceover reads, I usually have my eyes closed in order to fully concentrate on what I'm hearing. With Viola, I always pictured her speaking *at* me (not to me) from above with a distant, detached authority. She wasn't connecting with me as a listener, which meant that I had to work extra hard to focus on what she was trying to get across. When I relayed this feedback, she eventually confided long-term issues around being seen and heard which were rooted in a painful history with an abusive mother. It was a surprising and emotional moment for us both, and it explained so much about how she'd been approaching her reads.

Viola's experience of recognizing where this pattern came from (and having an emotional release about it) made an enormous difference in her subsequent performances. We also worked up a few strategies in case she reverted back to her old ways. She will still need to be vigilant until the new learning settles in, but she is now aware of the issue, understands its origins, and is equipped with a few solid tools to manage it.

Narrator Archetypes

From working with voice actors over many years, it's become clear that personal tendencies show up in performance with surprising regularity and predictability. There have been many times when I've been working with a new student, listened to them read a paragraph or two, then asked a question such as "Do you tend to be impatient?" or "Do you have a habit of analyzing everything?" In nearly every case, they react with a look that says "We just met, how could you possibly know that?" My answer is always the same: "It's in your read."

For example, narrators who are impatient (guilty, your honor) have a tendency to read very quickly or too far ahead. They stumble more often and lose energy at the ends of phrases and sentences as they're already focusing on the next line. Those who have a more analytical nature tend to overthink the text, mentally planning for and controlling every inflection and pause.

These patterns and others kept revealing themselves over and over again. I began to feel like some kind of crazy narration whisperer—identifying personality traits based on students' voiceover reads. It eventually occurred to me that distilling all this data into broadly defined narrator archetypes could prove useful. I reasoned that if a voice actor recognized themselves in an archetype, they could begin to understand some of the underlying causes of any performance issues and be better equipped to resolve them.

In looking through the narrator archetypes which follow, you may see yourself in one or more of them at the same time, and that's fine. After all, on a human level we're not the exact same person from day to day or even hour to hour. Life events, thoughts, actions, and our thoughts *about* those life events, thoughts, and actions perpetually color the lens through which we view our world. Naturally, this is going to affect everything we do, including how we communicate and perform.

Until we figure out how to be present and authentic at all times (no easy feat and probably what we're all here to learn) we could use a little help understanding and managing our mercurial nature and how it affects our performances.

The Manager

This is the gold standard for narration performance and the archetype we should all strive to model as often as possible. The Manager is thorough in their prep, remains present and focused during a read, and operates in a state of flow most of the time. They keep true to the intention they've set for the project and express themselves through a balance of mind, body, and voice. They use visualization, emotion, and gesture to read intuitively, lifting the text off the page and connecting fully with their listener. When they do veer off course, they are aware of it and know just what to do in order to get themselves back on track.

Managers are not infallible, but they have the internal and external skills required to consistently produce excellent performances and the ability to self-correct when necessary.

> The key to tapping into and maintaining the positive aspects of The Manager is:
> BALANCE.

The Analyzer

As you might imagine, this archetype is firmly rooted in the left brain. Analyzers have the impulse to mentally control every aspect of a voiceover performance, from inflection and pauses to melody, and even the tone of the voice. Analyzers are likely to map out an entire narration script beforehand which (as we have learned) doesn't always produce the most connected reads.

If you recognize yourself in this archetype, work on trusting yourself. I embodied this archetype for years and sterilized countless reads before I learned to relax, stop trying to control everything, and trust in my abilities and my prep.

Set your foundations carefully (especially your intention), make an effort to visualize, focus on connecting emotionally, and use gesture to bring the read into the body and away from your over-active mind. All of this will help you speak from the heart center and the intuitive right brain.

> The key to overcoming the negative aspects of The Analyzer is:
> TRUST.

The Worrier

As with The Analyzer, trust is an issue for this archetype, but The Worrier also struggles with confidence. In addition to concerns about delivering a good read, there are usually underlying issues with personal insecurity. Remember—we cannot separate who we are from how we communicate—but we can learn to become aware of our tendencies and develop strategies to overcome them during a performance.

If you recognize yourself in this archetype, working on your confidence in daily life will also improve your narration. Talk to other voice actors for support—ones who are at roughly the same skill level. You may be surprised to learn that they're having similar struggles. The best way to overcome the tendencies of The Worrier is simply to gain experience through practice and doing. With time, your confidence will grow and your worries will have less of a stranglehold.

> The key to overcoming the negative aspects
> of The Worrier is:
> CONFIDENCE.

The Perfectionist

I know this archetype well and we have a long history together. Even after decades of experience as a voice actor, I still have to be vigilant that it doesn't take me over.

As the name implies, The Perfectionist wants everything "just so." They have clear notions about the standard they're aiming for and are driven to achieve it at all costs. They listen to their own performance (*while* they're performing) and try to sanitize it as they go. The irony, of course, is that in trying to "perfect" the read, they actually cause it to unravel.

If you see yourself in this archetype, practice letting go of an impossible ideal. This does not mean you have to relax your standards (unconscionable to The Perfectionist) just shift your focus from "perfecting" to "expressing," then keep those tendencies at bay if you're also editing the audio.

> The key to overcoming the negative aspects
> of The Perfectionist is:
> LETTING GO.

The Monitor

This is another archetype I am very well acquainted with. If you saw yourself in The Perfectionist archetype, chances are you'll recognize yourself here as well.

The Monitor does just what the name suggests and listens too closely to what they're doing. They try to manage every aspect of the performance as it's happening and end up distracting themselves in the process. The more intensely they listen, the further they veer away from the flow; the further they veer away from the flow, the more intensely they listen (and judge what they hear). It's a vicious, self-conscious circle.

Here's a non-voiceover example of this cycle: if you've ever sat across from a mirror in a meeting room or taken part in a video call, you'll understand how challenging it can be to express yourself clearly with your reflection looking back at you. You talk a bit, get a glimpse of yourself, judge what you see, and start again. It's no different when the "reflection" is audio only.

The way to break out of this circular trap is to switch from "receive" to "transmit"—focus on expressing rather than listening (and judging). Also, refresh your foundations, tap into the feeling of the message, and get your body involved in the communication.

> The key to overcoming the negative aspects
> of The Monitor is:
> FOCUS.

The Bulldozer

The Bulldozer has a tendency to plow through narration text at full tilt, almost as if they can't wait to get it over with. These individuals are usually super driven in life and eager to finish whatever they're working on so they can move on to the next thing.

If you recognize yourself in this archetype, the first thing you need to do is *relax* and the second is to *enjoy* what you're doing. You wanted this job for a reason (hopefully it was slightly more for the love of the work than the monetary rewards) so have fun doing it. Approach your narration reads as though you wished they would never end.

> The key to overcoming the negative aspects
> of The Bulldozer is:
> PATIENCE.

The Anticipator

The Anticipator archetype has some aspects in common with The Analyzer, The Monitor, and The Bulldozer. The Anticipator sets their sights on the next important buzzword and rushes toward it, glossing over nearly everything in between. And they're not usually even aware that they're doing it. What drives this impulse is usually a mixture of the desire to plan ahead (The Analyzer) paying too much attention to the words and how they should be read (The Monitor) and being in a rush (The Bulldozer).

Over-anticipating what's ahead in the text can create pacing issues, an uneven read, and a higher stumbling rate. Whenever a student is exhibiting signs of The Anticipator, I use the analogy of driving on a winding road during a heavy fog—if you're thinking about how you'll handle two curves ahead, you'll miss the one you're on and probably crash.

If you recognize yourself in this archetype, concentrate on staying present and trusting that when the next buzzword appears, you'll instinctively know how to handle it.

> The key to overcoming the negative aspects
> of The Anticipator is:
> PRESENCE.

Please note that these archetypes are not set in stone. They are merely a collection of common narrator behaviors which have been observed and noted over the years. You may identify with one or more of them or perhaps none at all, and that's okay. You might display characteristics of one of them today and a different one next week, and that's okay too. And if your current habits do have you fitting neatly into a specific archetype, it doesn't mean that you're fated to be there forever—things can change in a heartbeat.

I've seen students who were really struggling, suddenly turn into proficient narrators, just with a simple change of focus. It's amazing what can happen when we start tinkering with how we communicate. Personal issues have a way of rising to the surface and once the spotlight of awareness shines on them, they can actually resolve themselves and transform us in the process. I've witnessed this many times and the outcome is not simply better voiceover performances, but a fundamental shift within the individual. This is what happened to a student during a narration workshop.

Transformation—Bella's Story

One of the first things I noticed about Bella was how soft spoken she was. Her voice was very quiet and had an almost apologetic quality to it. As she introduced herself and relayed to the group what she wanted to get from the day, I wondered if this was her authentic voice or if there was something else going on.

The first piece of copy we worked on together was a script for an online video, showcasing a beachfront vacation rental. I thought her soft tones would work well to encourage viewers to find out more about this holiday destination. Bella finished her first read-through and didn't feel particularly good about it. She was putting in a lot of effort, but because she was holding on so tightly to the idea of what the read should ultimately sound like, the result was a disconnected performance without heart. She was operating purely from her analytical mind and trying to mentally beat the read into submission.

After we listened back to the audio and discussed it a little, I asked how she expressed herself when she was out with her best friend. Her face lit up and she described a very different person from the one we had all met in the workshop. We invited that strong, confident woman to take part in Bella's performance.

Things were already beginning to shift when she had a lightbulb moment about bringing her Caribbean heritage into this read about an island paradise. The results were spectacular. Because she had tapped into an authentic facet of herself, she was able to make instinctive choices and the read completely came alive.

She was comfortable and confident, which allowed her to focus on the intention she had set for the piece (entice) and to express it fully without distraction.

What astonished the group even further was that this rediscovered, authentic Bella was with us for the rest of the day. From that turning point, her head was held high and her voice was strong with much more substance. Her accent even changed a little and now included a very slight Jamaican lilt.

Upon reflection, Bella reported that everyone had always told her that she had a "soft, sexy voice" and she had been buying into that and trying to live up to it for many years. She will still have access to that softer read when she needs it, but the real Bella is now firmly in the driver's seat.

3 **Projects**

There are many different subgenres of voiceover narration, each one requiring a slightly different mindset and approach. This chapter will serve as a glossary of sorts, providing information and foundational guidance about the most common types of narration project. Later, in Chapter 7, you'll have plenty of opportunities to practice with sample text, and I'll offer a few notes of assistance for each piece of copy, should you need them.

You will no doubt discover that you enjoy working on some narration projects more than others. Personally, I'm a bit partial to wordy medical scripts, heartfelt corporate messages, or any kind of e-learning, and less enthusiastic about audiobooks. Most people (students in particular) are surprised to learn this, and I usually explain it this way: I'm more of a sprinter than a marathon runner. I have a bouncy, impatient nature and find it difficult to sit still and focused for days at a time. In literary terms, I suppose you could say I'm more "Tigger" than "Pooh." But even though I was never all that keen on doing audiobooks, I still said "yes" whenever they were offered—until the day that I gave myself permission not to.

Several years ago, after a sweaty July week in my booth, I completed the last audiobook I've ever narrated. I was working remotely with a producer who did the recording. It was a challenging read, the booth was a sauna, and I felt like a squirmy child being forced to sit still in a sweltering church. When it was finally finished and I'd thanked the nice producer, I walked down the hall, looked at my reflection in the bathroom mirror, and said aloud "Sweetheart, I will never make you do that again."

For the longest time, I felt that I was *required* to take any and all voiceover jobs, as though it was part of some unwritten contract

I'd agreed to when I started my voice acting career. I figured it was just part of the gig that everyone must do—take whatever comes along in the hope that it will one day lead to something you enjoy—like eating your broccoli before you're allowed dessert.

But here's what I've learned: it really is okay if you're not enamored with every kind of narration project under the sun. Dancers don't usually love ballroom, ballet, *and* hip hop, do they? You're not in any way obligated to say "yes" to all of it. Sure, you can try a little of everything in the beginning to find out what you like and what you don't, but eventually you need to give yourself permission to focus on the jobs that you *enjoy*—the ones that light you up and really don't feel all that much like work. After all, the thought of a career doing something you love was probably part of what attracted you to voice acting in the first place, right? You're a grown-up—you can have your dessert without touching your broccoli.

Audiobooks

The audiobook industry has enjoyed a huge popularity spike in recent years, possibly because audiobooks are now much more accessible than ever. Long gone are the days of bulky folders filled with cassette tapes or CDs—now we just download an app, transfer the payment, and away we go.

While patrons of audiobooks obviously enjoy them, voice actors seem very much divided. Some narrators adore them and happily go from one project to the next. If they're not in the booth recording a book, they're reading, prepping, and creating the character voices to bring the next one to life. Others shy away from them, objecting to the lengthy prep time and the many hours it takes to record and edit them.

For those of you who *are* drawn to the world of audiobooks (and I hope my own proclivities haven't put you off) there is a veritable smorgasbord of projects out there which need skilled narrators, so if you feel the calling, just go for it. They do require more prep work than most other types of narration projects, so there's a special section in Chapter 4 dedicated to them.

Positioning

This will change depending on the project. You might have the role of impartial narrator telling the story or you might be portraying a character within that story as you tell it. In the case of a nonfiction book, you will most likely be speaking as an informed authority.

Intention

Your intention will vary depending on the type and style of the book. For example, a nonfiction book on PC repair might have an intention of "instructing" or "teaching," while a storybook for children between the ages of three and five would be more likely to have an intention of "entertaining" or "delighting."

Pace

Pace will depend on the genre or story. A general note for audiobooks is to go slower than you feel is necessary. As there are no accompanying visuals, you must allow time for the images to develop within the listeners' minds as the story unfolds or the information is presented.

Formality

The formality of an audiobook takes its cue from the genre and subject matter. For example, a nonfiction project about tackling world poverty is likely to be much more formal than one about origami or flower arranging.

Visuals

Because there are no accompanying visuals for audiobooks (outside of the listeners' minds) your narration performance takes center stage. The responsibility of telling the story (or conveying the information in the case of a nonfiction book) rests completely with you and your delivery.

Audio Description (AD)

I'm not particularly proud to admit that I once thought of audio description (AD) as a poor relation to voice acting. I figured it was best left to the novice who hasn't yet learned all the tricks of the trade. How wrong I was!

In case you're unfamiliar with it, AD is a service for the visually impaired. Voiceover segments (called descriptions) are placed between character dialogue in a film, television show, or live theater, and they describe any action that may otherwise be missed by a visually impaired viewer. AD can also be used in museums to describe an exhibition or individual works of art. It's delicate work to get it just right.

As fate would have it, I had some pre-training in AD when I was a teenager. My lovely little grandma Bernice lost her sight when she was around forty years old. She was a 4'11" firecracker and could do almost anything a sighted person could do (except maybe drive). Whenever we watched television together, I would help her out by explaining what was happening on the screen. She was fine when characters were speaking or when there was an obvious action sequence (such as a car chase) but she needed to have some of the gaps filled in so she could follow the story. For instance, I would need to tell her when a scene changed from day to night, if a character reacted without words, or a cowboy silently entered the saloon wearing a gun a menacing look. I got a kick out of doing this for her and had no idea it would come in so handy all these years later.

Blending with the orchestra

In the last chapter, we covered how a narration read supports or supplements any visuals, which are the star of the show. With most types of AD (films, television, and theater) the narration sits even further out of the limelight, so as not to be overwhelming. The visually impaired audience is already taking in several streams of input, all of which are audio: speaking characters, the sounds of what's happening, and the mood-setting music underneath it all. That's a lot of information to sort through without the benefit of the visual elements. AD adds yet another audio element to all that, so it must be unobtrusive.

If your performance is too big, it will overpower the experience; too flat or detached, and it will be distracting. For example, if the scene to be described is a woman being chased through the woods by a homicidal maniac, you cannot choose a deadpan delivery to say "Kate is in the woods running for her life."You must allow the drama and tension of the moment to come through in your voice, without upstaging everything else. Think of a good AD performance as providing another instrument to blend with the orchestra in order to paint pictures in the listeners' minds.

AD is not the most lucrative area of voiceover, but it's satisfying work knowing that you're providing a valuable service to enhance the experience of a visually impaired viewer.

Positioning

The AD narrator is impartial and never part of the story. To help you get a sense of the right tone and delivery, think of a golf commentator on the radio. Their job is to report all the sporting action to those listening who cannot see the players or the course. They have to convey a sense of occasion without being too overpowering. When something unexpected happens, they need to be able to share the emotion of the moment without distracting the golfers or the other spectators.

Intention

The intention for AD is always to "describe." The narrator's role is to explain what is happening, supplement what is being heard, and enhance the enjoyment of the viewer.

Pace

The pace for AD varies depending on what action is taking place and how tightly written the descriptions are. The text needs to fit between character dialogue, but there may be some pivotal action which needs to be explained in a short space of time, so that description would need to be read more quickly.

Formality

AD falls toward the informal end of the scale. It's more like a friend explaining the action than an outside authority conveying information.

Visuals

The visuals will be the film, television program, live theater, or artwork. But unlike other types of narration project, the visuals for AD will obviously not be the primary focus.

Audio Guides (Audio Tours)

Visitors to a large museum or exhibition will often have the option of using a recorded audio guide, which is available in a variety of languages. This is usually in the form of a handheld device, headset, or app, and is designed to guide the visitor through the space, provide additional information, or otherwise enhance their experience.

Most of the time, an audio guide will be comprised of the narrator's voice on its own (and possibly some music) to accompany the patron throughout their visit, so the performance needs to be intimate as well as informative. Other times, it can be a larger production with various characters guiding and entertaining the visitor.

Positioning

For a straight audio guide read, your point of view will usually be as a representative of the museum or exhibition organizers. You are speaking on their behalf to make the visitors' experience a pleasant one.

Intention

The intention for audio guides will nearly always be to guide, inform, or explain.

Pace

The pace for an audio guide will usually be on the slower side. Visitors to a museum are rarely in a hurry and, as they are learning as well, you want to give them time to take in the information and enjoy what they are experiencing.

Formality

The formality for audio guides depends on the project. They can range from very formal to conversational, or even lighthearted. Others may also require characters for the production.

Visuals

While the performance itself is audio only, your read will need to blend with and enhance the visuals of the museum or exhibition.

Corporate Films

This is a very broad area of voiceover narration. The term "corporate" is used as a catch-all for various types of organizational projects including product launches, recruitment films, and productions about a company's policies, products, or services.

Positioning

Your point of view for a corporate film will vary depending on the project. You may be speaking as a member of the company, an outside authority, or a character within the production.

Intention

The underlying motivation for most corporate films is to sell. This is true whether it's a brand, a new product, service, or a revolutionary idea. But as a general rule, you don't want the intention of "selling" to drive your narration. Look for the subtlety behind the sell. For example, a recruitment film for a software company may well be intending to sell prospective employees on the merits of the company, but a more refined intention for your read might be to "convince" or "entice."

Pace

One of the most efficient ways to establish the tempo for a corporate narration read is to hear the music bed, and if you can listen to it *while* you're narrating, that's even better. The pace and mood then become instinctive. If the production music hasn't been chosen yet or isn't available, ask the producer what they have in mind so you can at least get a sense of what pace would be appropriate.

Another production factor which will affect pace is the visuals. They may have already been filmed, edited, and approved by four levels of corporate management, which means that your voiceover needs to be shoehorned in afterward, and it's not always a perfect fit. Your challenge will be to deliver the read within the allotted time without compromising the quality of the client's message.

Formality

Formality in a corporate film could be anything from deadly serious to lighthearted and fun. It really depends on the company and the particular project.

Visuals

The visuals for a corporate project could be a film or video shot on location, in front of a green screen, created from a collection of stock footage, a series of still images, or an animation.

Documentaries

Documentaries are factual films, usually intended to educate and/or entertain. There are as many different documentary styles as there are subjects, so approaches to narrating them will vary greatly.

Positioning

The point of view for most documentary narration will be as an outside authority.

Intention

Common intentions for documentaries would be to inform, educate, teach, or entertain.

Pace

Pace will vary greatly depending on the subject matter and production. For example, if you had two documentaries about famous bands, one about The Carpenters and the other about Queen, the pace and feel would likely be very different.

Formality

The formality level for corporate narration projects depends on the target audience and the subject matter.

E-learning

E-learning can be used to teach any number of topics from using new software to a company's health and safety practices. For most e-learning projects, your audience will be one person at a computer, who will be learning online or using a stand-alone program or app. They will have your voice in their ears for an extended period of time, so the read has to be authentic and personal. Narration reads which are intended for an audience of one have a different quality to them than those directed toward a group. This is where visualizing that person can bring the necessary subtlety and nuance to the read.

Positioning

For e-learning projects, you will usually be speaking as a representative of the company.

Intention

Your intention for e-learning will almost always be to teach, educate, or instruct.

Pace

The pace of e-learning is generally on the slower side to allow time for the listener to take in the information and study whatever visuals are being shown.

Formality

The formality for e-learning depends on the subject matter. For example, an e-learning module about a company's disciplinary policies would probably be more serious and formal than one about its annual social functions.

Visuals

The visuals for an e-learning project could take various forms: animation, live action, or a screenshot of an app or program on a computer screen.

Explainer Videos

These are basically "how to" films on any number of subjects, from re-wiring a house to assembling a child's cuckoo clock.

Positioning

Narrators for explainer videos are most often speaking as a representative of the company.

Visuals

Visuals for explainer videos can be just about anything: live action, a series of still images, or animation. They will usually show a demonstration of some kind.

Intention

As the name would suggest, the intention is usually to explain or instruct.

Pace

The pace for an explainer video is on the slower side. The viewer will be learning and possibly doing something at the same time—assembling a recent purchase, for example—so the pacing needs room to breathe to give the viewer time to take it all in.

Formality

The formality level for explainer videos will depend on the client and the subject matter. For example, a production explaining how to put together a children's bicycle will likely be much less formal than one demonstrating how to operate a piece of life-saving medical equipment.

Holiday Video Tours

Holiday video tours are films used to promote a specific holiday destination. They can be produced for group viewings or for online use, such as on a company's website or social media platforms.

Positioning

The narrator's point of view for a holiday video tour is most often as a representative of the company.

Visuals

The visuals usually consist of video and/or stills of the vacation spot.

Intention

The intention for holiday video tours is nearly always to entice. The objective is to encourage potential buyers to either make a booking on the spot or to learn more.

Pace

The pace for a holiday video tour would take its cue from the other production elements (visuals and music) and from the nature of the destination. For example, a video for a relaxing vacation by a secluded lake would have a different feel and pace than one for a white-water rafting holiday.

Formality

The formality level depends on the company and the subject matter.

Interactive Voice Recordings (IVR)

Interactive Voice Recordings are company telephone greetings with multiple choice options (for sales, press one; for accounts, press two). IVRs are, in effect, a digital receptionist.

Positioning

The point of view for IVR recordings is always as a member of the company.

Visuals

No visuals.

Intention

The overriding intentions are to inform and direct.

Pace

The pace for IVR is generally on the slower side, especially if the company receives international calls.

Formality

As IVRs are essentially recorded company greetings, the formality level would match that of an actual receptionist for that particular organization. The tone is usually warm, but business-like.

Language Training (LT)

Until you get the hang of them, LT projects can be a little tricky. The reason for this is that your performance has to work on multiple levels. The text itself, which is usually a series of short lessons and exercises (stories, character dialog, radio interviews, and so on) sits within the overall project, the purpose of which is to teach a language to non-native speakers. In addition, each mini-script has specific learning objectives which need to be brought out in the read. I'll give you an example.

Let's say you're narrating a project which will be used to teach Level 5 English to ten-year-old children and one of the modules contains copy for a radio show intro. Let's also say that the purpose of this piece is to teach the students about different pronunciations of words containing "ough" (such as trough, thought, and thorough). Your narration read will need to balance several aspects: a decent read of the radio intro, keeping the pace appropriate for Level 5 learners, and an emphasis on the words which are the feature of the lesson (trough, thought, and thorough). It can be a lot to juggle, but it's not difficult once you get used to it. Two important tips for working on a LT project are:

1. Enunciate more than you feel is necessary.
2. Resist the urge to speed up.

Positioning

This varies depending on the scripts within each module. You could be playing any number of characters, or have the role of impartial narrator, introducing each module and reading the titles.

Visuals

If there are any visuals, they will usually be the images in the students' workbooks.

Intention

Of course, the overall intention will be to teach, but each section of text within the project will have its own specific intention.

To be honest, it's rare to get this type of script in advance, so there won't be time for much foundational work before you record. This is one of those times when you'll have to rely on your instincts and intuition.

Pace

The pace for LT is usually based on the learning level. For example, a read for English Level 1 will be extremely slow and deliberate (and takes focus and concentration to maintain) whereas Level 5 would be closer to a natural pace.

Formality

The formality level for LT will vary depending on the text and the level being taught.

Medical

Medical films are generally produced as an educational tool for students and professionals. But some projects are produced for patients—for example, to explain the benefits and risks of a clinical trial or the side effects of a prescribed medication. The subject matter could be anything medically related.

Positioning

The point of view for medical narration is often as an outside authority, but could be from a company's perspective as well, such as the launch of a new medication.

Visuals

Quite often, the visuals for medical films are animation (3D is common) but they could also be live action, video, film, or a combination of these.

Intention

The intention is usually to inform, educate, or teach.

Pace

The pace will depend on the project, but medical reads are generally on the slower side as their content can be heavy.

Formality

Medical reads are usually quite formal as the target audience is often medically trained professionals. A notable exception would be a video for participants in a clinical trial. Narration for this type of project tends to be a little warmer to reassure the patient.

Museum Display

In addition to an audio guide in a museum or exhibition, there could also be an audio/visual component within a display, which either tells a story or provides additional information about the surrounding artifacts. This could be in the form of a video monitor showing a narrated film on a loop, an audio production of a historical event, or simply the voices of historical figures to add atmosphere to the exhibit.

Positioning

Usually, the role in one of these productions is either an impartial narrator or a specific character within a production.

Visuals

The visuals could be anything, depending on the production and what's being shown. They might be part of a film showing on a monitor, a series of stills with narration behind it, or perhaps something moving within the display (a machine, for example) with audio to explain what's being seen.

Intention

Common intentions for this type of project would be to educate, teach, or entertain.

Pace

The pace for museum display narration varies depending on the project (and whether characters are part of it) but is generally on the slower side. As with the audio guide, those who visit museums are rarely in a hurry.

Formality

The formality level depends on the subject matter.

On Hold Messaging

Audio is also often used to inform customers about products and services while they are on hold and waiting for a company representative. On hold messaging could be considered a kind of "audio billboard." It takes advantage of the extra time available to speak to a customer who is holding. The messages are basically a series of short commercials, usually interspersed with apologies for keeping their customers waiting.

Positioning

The point of view for on hold messaging is always as a member of the company. It would seem very odd to call a company and have the voice tell you that "Company X is glad you called and they will be with you in a moment."

Visuals

On hold work is audio only.

Intention

The overriding intention is to placate—to keep the caller happy while they wait (and make sure they're happy *to* wait). As the company has a captive audience, this is also the perfect time to sell products and services. Additional intentions might be to entice, convince, or excite.

Pace

The pace for on hold messaging is generally on the slower side. The object is usually to keep callers calm and engaged while they wait, so a moderately paced read is usually a solid choice.

Formality

The formality level depends on the nature of the company, the products or services they offer, and the nature of the clientele. For example, the on hold messaging for Tammy's Party Supplies would be much less formal than that of Larry's Funeral Home.

Point-of-Sale Videos

Point-of-sale videos are short films about a company's products or services, which are usually played out on small screens close to where the item can be purchased. These projects can either be high energy and punchy to attract attention in a crowded store or on the subtler side, for example, showcasing the newest bestseller in a bookstore.

Positioning

The point of view is nearly always as of a member of the company.

Visuals

Visuals are commonly live action demonstrations, but they could be a mixture of anything.

Intention

The purpose of point-of-sale videos is obviously to sell something. However, a more refined intention for the narration might be to amaze, persuade, or tempt.

Pace

The pace depends on what's being sold and the surroundings where the video is placed. A video produced to sell memory foam pillows for that perfect, restful night's sleep is going to be much slower paced than one to sell a gadget that chops, peels, slices, and dices.

Formality

The formality for point-of-sale videos depends on the product and the target audience, but is usually more informal and friendly, to draw in customers.

Satellite Navigation (Satnav)

While your intention will certainly be "guiding," satnav is a very different animal from say, a museum guide. In essence, you are lending a human voice to a mechanical system, so you won't be striving for connection with the listener—just giving them directions and information.

Satnav is a sub-genre where focusing on precision in your performance is actually necessary. You'll need to carefully manage your intonation so that the different elements can be edited together and sound fluent.

You won't be recording every possible combination of words and numbers. What you do is record all of the lines which will contain a number and then leave a gap for them. The numbers are then read separately with the correct intonation and pitch so they can be slotted in as seamlessly as possible. If you're musically inclined or have a good ear, this will be a great help for narrating a satnav system.

Positioning

The positioning for satnav is impartial—in fact, even beyond "impartial"—as the human element of the read is all but eliminated.

Visuals

The only visuals will be the map on the screen. Visuals do not need to be taken into account for a satnav read.

Intention

The intention for satnav will always be guiding, directing, and informing.

Pace

While there are no time constraints on the read for a satnav system, clarity is important, which usually slows down the read.

Formality

A satnav read will generally be very formal (unless it's a novelty project such as a celebrity sound-alike or character). The read is more like an approximation of a computer voice and is one of the few instances where connection with the audience is not an objective.

Technical

Technical narration encompasses those projects containing specialized language, usually meant for an audience who is highly skilled in a specific area.

Positioning

The point of view depends on the project, and could be an outside authority or a member of an organization.

Visuals

The visuals can vary greatly, depending on the project. They could be live action, a series of still images, animation, or any combination of these.

Intention

The overall intentions for technical scripts would be to educate, teach, or instruct. However, it's always better to identify the most refined intention for each project, for example, demonstrate, elucidate, or caution.

Pace

The pace will depend on the subject matter, but will generally be on the slower end of the spectrum. By their very nature, technical projects can contain complex language and ideas, so a slower pace is usually preferred.

Formality

The formality level for a technical script will depend on the project, but will generally be quite formal, given their specialized nature and audience.

4 **Prep**

Now that you have an understanding of the driving forces of human communication, the foundations of a good spoken word performance, and an overview of the most common project types, we can finally start folding all of this knowledge and wisdom into the actual mechanics of voiceover narration. As with any performance skill, good narration begins with good preparation. Here are the three main steps:

1. Set your foundations.
2. Prepare the text.
3. Prepare your mind, body, and voice.

When you're booked for a narration project, you will usually do your script work in advance (a day or so before you record) which means that your various stages of prep will be spread across different days. For our purposes, in order to keep the different aspects of prep guidance together in one place, we'll work on the assumption that it will all happen just before you record.

Some projects take longer to prep, such as lengthy e-learning projects and audiobooks. At the end of the chapter, there is a special section dedicated to prepping audiobooks, including creating the character voices which will bring them to life.

Pouring the Foundations

As we discussed at length in Chapter 2, setting your foundations before you begin narrating helps you create an authentic, well-rounded, and connected read. This important first step streamlines your delivery and enhances your performance in a number of ways:

1. Paves the way for a more authentic performance.
2. Frees you to focus more on expression than the words.
3. Gives your read a natural flow.
4. Makes you far less likely to stumble.

With a little practice, working out the foundational elements for a read will become second nature and you'll be able to do it almost instantly. In time, you'll be able to simply look at a piece of copy and know instinctively what to do with it. Until then, you may find that a worksheet comes in handy. Use the Foundations Worksheet provided, or create one of your own—whatever works best for you.

Foundations Worksheet

Who am I? Who am I talking to?   What do I want from the audience?

Positioning What is my role as the narrator?	Company Representative Outside Authority Other_____

The 3 Dials: *Intention*: (refer to the List of Intentions in Chapter 2) *Pace*: 1–10 (1 = very slow) *Formality*: 1–10 (1= very informal)	 1 2 3 4 5 6 7 8 9 10 1 2 3 4 5 6 7 8 9 10

Visuals: What else could I visualize in order to enhance the read?	Film, animation, stills, screen capture Other_____

Notes on emotional set-point:

Notes on gesturing:

Any other performance notes:

Preparing the Text

We've discussed at length how creating a "road map" of every inflection, pause, and breath is really not the best way to approach a narration read. That being said, I guarantee that there will be jobs where you'll at least need a few "signposts" to help guide you through.

Many times, you'll be presented with text so beautifully written that you can just set your foundations and walk on down the road, so to speak. Other times, the copy will be complex, oddly translated, or just poorly written (sorry, but it happens), and rather than a nice easy stroll on level ground with clear visibility, you'll be climbing a steep, rocky embankment in stilettos and a ski mask. With projects like these, it can be helpful to add a little script notation to your foundational prep.

To be clear, using notation to simplify the delivery of a difficult script is not the same as notating every utterance you plan to make during a read. There is a very important distinction here: one helps to free you from the analytical mind; the other traps you in it.

Notation

Notation can be any kind of mark you like, as long as it makes sense to you during the read and it doesn't cause you to think about it. Here are some simple notation tools that I use:

1. "/" divides a long sentence or paragraph into separate thoughts.

2. ( ) marks a less important phrase. When you're in the middle of a read, parentheses help you see in a split second that everything within them is a side note and you'll know instinctively how to deliver it. It's also a good way to break up overwritten sentences.

3. [ ] groups word strings together. I use this notation often and it's a lifesaver for complicated text. When you're immersed in a complex read, your eyes recognize very quickly that everything within the square brackets is essentially one thing, which keeps you from getting lost in awkward sentences.

Consider this extract from an extremely technical script:

The primary set of 24 coupling rods are directly connected to the drive belt assembly by 110 ct. 1-7/16" heavy hex bolts and covered by a direct-line series of 12' diameter steel plates, which protect the shaft and coupling rods as well as the transfer valve from wear and tear during normal operation. The protective panels surrounding the piston housing and cylinder assembly must be checked in accordance with the approved maintenance schedule, must comply with sections 6.2, 6.3 and 6.4 of the Safety Code and be replaced when a) rust is visible on or around the panels; b) the rivets have become damaged, worn or knocked off center as a result of normal or abnormal operation; or c) any part of a panel has been visibly oxidized by humidity or inconsistent ambient temperature, in accordance with regulation 45(a) of the 1996 Code of Operation Standards (COS). In the event that the piston housing assembly becomes unstable or exhibits abnormal vibrations over 10% above the level certified upon installation, consult pages 528–561 of the maintenance manual or contact the engineering team for a consult.

This is some very thorny text and appears to have been lifted straight from a technical manual. It was clearly not written for the spoken word (which happens more often than you might think). The first thing to do with copy like this is to find out how the client would like the terms to be read. Then you can make a few notes to help smooth out the read. Let's say that we have already clarified the following terms with the client:

110 = a hundred and ten

ct. = count

1-7/16" = one and seven sixteenths inch

12' = twelve foot

45(a) = forty-five A

COS = C-O-S

528–561 = five-two-eight to five-six-one

It's a good idea to note this direction within the text, whether it's on paper or a tablet. Having the information on a separate sheet/screen or relying on memory can be distracting, pushing you further into your head.

Here's what the first part of the prepared text might look like, with the notation in bold:

> *The primary set of 24 coupling rods are directly connected to the drive belt assembly by 110* ~~ct.~~ **count** *1-7/16"* **(one and seven sixteenths inch)** *heavy hex bolts and covered by a* [*direct-line series of 12'* **(foot)** *diameter steel plates*]*, which protect the shaft and coupling rods as well as the transfer valve from wear and tear during normal operation. The* [*protective panels surrounding the piston housing and cylinder assembly*] *must be checked.*

Rather than spelling out 1-7/16" in words, you could write "and" above the hyphen, circle 7/16 (as long as you would instinctively say it correctly) and write "inch" somewhere so you wouldn't be tempted to say "inches." Use the simplest notation you can to quickly remind yourself of the preferences. Try different things and find what works best for you.

Notice the text which has been surrounded by [ ]. By placing square brackets around [direct-line series of 12' diameter steel plates] and [protective panels surrounding the piston housing and the cylinder assembly] your eyes now see each of those word strings as one thing, which simplifies the text and makes it easier to decipher at speed.

Let's look at the next part of the copy:

> *The protective panels surrounding the piston housing and cylinder assembly must be checked in accordance with the approved maintenance schedule, must comply with sections 6.2, 6.3 and 6.4 of the Safety Code and be replaced when a) rust is visible on or around the panels; b) the rivets have become damaged, worn or knocked off center as a result of normal or abnormal operation; or c) any part of a panel has been visibly oxidized by humidity or inconsistent ambient temperature, in accordance with regulation 45(a) of the 1996 Code of Operation Standards (COS).*

> *In the event that the piston housing assembly becomes unstable or exhibits abnormal vibrations over 10% above the level certified upon installation, consult pages 528–561 of the maintenance manual or contact the engineering team for a consult.*

Notice that the highlighted section is one long sentence and it's a real mouthful. I would be tempted to suggest a minor script change here and create a new sentence after "maintenance schedule":

> *The protective panels surrounding the piston housing and cylinder assembly must be checked in accordance with the approved maintenance schedule. They must comply with . . .*

For the page numbers 528–561, I would just underline each digit and write "to" above the dash. If they decided that they wanted it read as "five twenty-eight" instead, then I would underline "twenty-eight" as a quick reminder to group them this way (e.g., 5<u>28</u>).

There are no set rules about notation and after a while, you'll develop your own personal style which doesn't need to make sense to anyone else. Its sole purpose is to free you from having to make mental decisions while you're in the flow of a read. Use notation sparingly and only as either a quick reminder of the director's notes or as a streamlining tool (like the square brackets). As for punctuation, feel free to tweak it within a script to help it flow for you. Unless it actually changes the meaning, there's no need to even mention it.

Preparing Mind, Body, and Voice

As we've discussed in previous chapters, it is crucial that your MBV work together as a team. Over time and with practice, you'll discover what works best for you in order to get your trio aligned and ready to narrate. In the meantime, here are some suggestions to get you started.

Mind

Meditation

There are many different forms of meditation and if you are already familiar with one or more, that's great. If you're not, don't worry (and try not to let the word "meditation" put you off). It may help to think of meditation as simply focusing your awareness—a way of becoming sharp and calm so that you can narrate unencumbered.

Even a very basic meditation can be useful to center yourself before a performance. Try this to begin: sit with your eyes closed and focus on your breathing for three minutes. Whenever your mind wanders, gently pull it back to the breath. That's it. It may not feel like you're doing much, but this very simple practice will help to get you out of your head, while bringing a sense of calm and focus.

Meditation isn't about ceasing all thought, it's about (in part) reaching a level of awareness where the thoughts you do have pass through you without getting snagged and spiraling out of control.

Visualization

In Chapter 2, I wrote extensively on the benefits of visualization while you're narrating. If your project has accompanying visuals, ask to see them. If this isn't possible, find something else to visualize to ensure your performance is well-rounded and blends seamlessly with the finished images.

I should also point out that if you're working on a project without visuals (such as an audiobook) visualizing who you're reading to can be very beneficial.

Body

For most narration jobs, you won't be gearing up for vigorous physical exercise. Nevertheless, you'll still want to make sure that your whole body is ready to be involved in the performance, even if you're going to be sitting down the entire time.

Stretching

Stretching is a great way of inviting your body to the party. No one knows better than you where your body holds tension, so just pay attention and stretch accordingly. Personally, my shoulders and neck are my main trouble spots, so I do my best to make sure everything is nice and loose before settling into the booth. Here are a few simple stretches you can do to help get your body performance-ready:

1. Let your head fall forward (don't force it) and feel the stretch in the upper back and neck. Rotate your head gently from side to side.
2. Roll your shoulders forward and back.

3. Rotate your wrists and ankles.

4. Stretch out the muscles in your thighs and calves.

If you don't have time to do a proper physical warm-up, at least stretch your facial muscles. I do this before every session without fail, and it only takes a minute:

1. Open your mouth as wide as it will go. Keeping your lips pulled back, move your jaw up and down a few times and then from side to side.

2. Stretch your upper and lower lips around your teeth a few times.

3. Keeping your mouth closed, fill each cheek with air to stretch them out, and then do the same with the space between both lips and your teeth.

4. Stretch out your entire face by mouthing the word "wow." Over-enunciate and get your eyelids and eyebrows moving.

By doing these exercises, you'll be stretching out your expression muscles and this can really make a difference to a read. Try this: record a little something first thing in the morning, run through the stretches, then record again. You should hear a marked improvement in clarity.

Getting Heart-centered

In previous chapters, we've explored how harmonizing the heart and brain can strengthen your intuition and improve your narration reads. I also promised to show you a way that you can do this.

While this particular exercise won't be everyone's cup of tea, I suggest you try it at least once. You may be surprised at how effective it can be to shift your focus away from the analytical mind and help you deliver a more authentic spoken word performance.

This heart-centering meditation is ancient and combines mental, physical, and energetic elements to stimulate the energy of the heart. It starts with hand placement on the body: place your right hand on the heart center (the middle of the sternum, near the heart) with your left hand on top, and the tips of the thumbs touching. This physical action begins the meditation from the level of the body (awareness follows touch). Now visualize your hands emitting bright light— infusing gratitude, compassion, and reverence. You may already be able to feel a slight shift.

Three points of focus are then used to move this energy: touch, awareness, and mantra, the last of which is based on the four attributes of the heart center. Say each one aloud to call them in: compassion, innate harmony (calm in the midst of chaos), healing presence, and unconditional love.

You don't need to be still during this meditation, so if your body wants to move in response to shifting energy, then just allow it to do so. If your mind wanders, gently bring it back to the breath, the attribute, and the sense of touch on your heart center. Doing this practice for ten minutes each day is suggested in order to keep your heart center open.[1]

Voice

Your voice should be warmed up before any type of vocal performance, but the method you use is a personal choice. Something I like to do is sing and harmonize with a few favorite songs. It not only warms up my voice, but it calms me, and there's something about doing vocal harmony which brings me into balance.

There is a huge array of vocal exercises and advice available on how to care for your voice. Explore what's out there and find what feels right and works best for you. In the meantime, here is an abbreviated four-part vocal warm-up, courtesy of top voice coach, Yvonne Morley:[2]

Physical preparation (tension release):

1. Shoulders (rolls, shrugs).
2. Neck (hang your head down, move in half-circles between your shoulders).
3. Jaw (relax open and say "yah yah yah" and repeat as needed).

Breath preparation (abdominal release):

1. Breathe all the way out on a long "SHHH" (your tummy should firm/tighten).
2. Relax and breathe in again (your tummy should soften/expand slightly).

Vocal preparation (vocal range and resonance):

1. Lip trilling up and down your range.
2. Gently hum to feel vibration (with a hand) in upper chest, throat, nose, and face.

Speech preparation (articulation):

1. "Big chewing" to move lips, cheeks, nose, chin, and eyebrows.

Rehearsing

Rehearsal has always been the standard way to prepare for any kind of performance. A stage actor can't just memorize their lines and then hop on stage for the opening night. They must go over it and over it, blending all aspects of the performance until it coalesces and becomes part of them.

With voiceover, it's a whole different ballgame. One of the big differences is that the stage actor isn't directed in real time. They will have had their rehearsal period with the director, who prepared them to fly solo. The voice actor, on the other hand, prepares only up to a point and then works with the director to guide the performance home. If narration copy is rehearsed too much, the performance starts to congeal, which makes altering it during the session more difficult.

Here's what I've learned about over-rehearsing: Of course you want to be prepared, but if you practice too much before a session, you risk becoming undirectable. You want to be familiar enough with the text and how the performance feels, without letting a specific read get too ingrained. Set your foundations, work your narration into reasonable shape, and then leave it alone. The goal is to present a decent first read which is then available for tweaking by the director.

If you're recording alone and not working with a director, then you are in charge of leading the rehearsal. Find a way of working that suits you and brings out your best performance. Here's what I do to prepare when I'm flying solo:

1. Read the copy silently to myself.
2. Set my foundations.
3. Read the copy aloud, but under my breath.
4. Rehearse once or twice in full performance mode.

Something to keep in mind when rehearsing for self-records: Be aware of your pace. During a rehearsal, it's really easy to read much more quickly than you intend to for the actual recording. But what happens is that your narration machinery takes the rehearsal at face value and calibrates to whatever you're feeding it. If you must speed-read as part of your rehearsal process (and it's a good way to get out of your head) do a couple of takes at the correct pace before you record as a kind of "vocal palate cleanser."

Prep for Audiobooks

Narrating audiobooks is not for the faint-hearted. I think you really have to love them in order to do them well. For starters, you're signing up for a marathon, not a sprint—it's a big commitment. Of all the subgenres of narration, the most labor intensive (and some say the most rewarding) is audiobooks. There will be days of reading and prep to complete and you may even have to go through the book more than once before you feel ready to record. But the upside is getting to immerse yourself in a story or subject and draw the listener into it, using nothing but the words on the page and your own storytelling skills. As mentioned in the previous chapter, you will probably either be drawn to narrate audiobooks or repelled by the thought of them.

Shifting foundations

The approach for audiobook prep differs from that of other types of narration projects. Setting your foundations is still an important first step, though the components are slightly different. And some (which we covered in Chapter 2) won't apply at all. I'll take you through some of the key differences and follow up with a tailored foundations worksheet.

For audiobooks, you still need to know who you are and who you're talking to. Are you an impartial narrator telling the story, a character within that story, or something else? Take a moment to consider your role, as well as the genre, who the audience is for that type of audiobook, and what they might want to experience when they listen to it. For instance, if you're narrating a battle-filled space epic for hardcore sci-fi fans, they'll be looking for a very different ride than someone listening to a Henry James novel.

Setting your intention is still beneficial for audiobook prep, though you may wish to have several—perhaps a primary choice for the book as a whole, then separate ones for each chapter, if necessary. Once again, be sure to be as specific as you can when choosing your intentions.

While setting an intention will be beneficial to your audiobook prep, the pace and formality dials won't be all that useful. Your pace will be dictated by the story (and the emotional content within it) and, as the only visuals will be those in the listeners' minds, your read won't need to align with any pre-edited images or timings, so it can be much freer. As for the formality dial, you might still consider it for a nonfiction project (a book on how to make paper roses would be much less formal than one on how to survive a divorce) but for fiction, it's not much use.

Audiobook Foundations Worksheet

Fiction or nonfiction?	
Genre (science fiction, romance, historical, etc.)	

Positioning

What is my role as the storyteller?	Impartial narrator
	Character within the story
	Other_____
What can be said about the potential audience? (sci-fi fans, history buffs, romantics, students, etc.)	
How will this knowledge affect the style and feel of my read?	

Intention

(refer to the List of Intentions in Chapter 2)

Additional Notes

This is a short foundations worksheet for audiobook prep. If you find it helpful, feel free to use it. If not, you can alter it to suit your needs or disregard it altogether.

Characters

Character voice is one element of audiobook work which is not seen all that often in the broader world of narration, but every novel on the planet has characters that will need to be brought to life— to leap off the page and into the listeners' imaginations. Character voice creation and performance is a comprehensive subject and one worthy of an entire book on its own, but for your work as an audiobook narrator, you need to at least understand the basics.

The first thing you should know is that most audiobooks won't require fully fledged characters—just suggestions of them. The main reason is that the listener already knows that each of the characters will be portrayed by the same person (in books with a single narrator) so the reader just needs to make it clear when someone else is speaking. Don't get me wrong—your characters still need to be good! They should be well-performed and consistent, but unless you're narrating a children's book (which usually require total characterization and then some), it won't usually be necessary to go "full-on Meryl Streep" with them. Think of the character voices in audiobooks as watercolors, rather than the vibrant oils of those in animation or video games.

Of course, there are exceptions to this watercolor-character school of thought. A producer or author may request that the character voices be fully developed in order to come across more true to life. Interestingly, I have read listener comments about this and many are not fans, preferring instead to let the characters develop and live in their own imagination—the way *they* choose to bring them to life.

At the end of the day, the level of characterization in an audiobook is up to the people who have hired you, so you'll need to craft your performance around their vision for the project.

Character Casting

My friend Ana, who is a successful audiobook narrator, recently reminded me of a character technique which is pure gold. Rather than creating her character voices from scratch, she "casts" them from real people. She doesn't necessarily need to know them personally—just have a sense of who they are and what they sound like. For example, when she needs a strong, deep-voiced American woman, she brings Angelina Jolie to mind. If she needs a salty old character from Northern England, then Great Uncle Henry gets the gig. This is a really useful way to create character voices, and one that is often used in animation (you may have noticed characters in *The Simpsons* who sound a little bit like JFK or Walter Matthau).

Using this method for audiobook characters has nothing to do with the quality of the impression and everything to do with anchoring the character, giving it roots and consistency. For instance, if my friend's "American lady" appears in the opening chapter and then goes away until chapter nine, she doesn't need to flounder, trying to remember what that character sounded like, or how she produced the voice—she simply goes back to the source, and calls Ms. Jolie back to the microphone.

Character Separation

Whether you cast your audiobook characters from real people or create them from scratch, it's important to make sure that they sound and feel different enough from each other, especially if they appear together in the book. This is known as *character separation*.

One of the last audiobooks I narrated had multiple scenes with half a dozen 17-year-old girls all talking to one another. It was a challenge to find character voices with enough separation that the listener could tell them apart, especially when there were no clarifications such as "Debbie said" or "Sandra said" to clue them in. As their ages and attitudes were all so similar, accents and vocal attributes came to the rescue.

Accents

Although I had to stay true to any accent already established in the narrative, I was free to assign different ones to the minor characters in the group of teens. I started by making a note of the girls who spoke to each other without being named. These characters would need the most separation in their voices so that the listener could easily follow the scene. For those moments, I chose strong accents to sit next to each other (like Texas and Minnesota) and then decided on the other accents from there.

If you want to narrate novels, developing your ability to do different accents is a must. I wouldn't want to prescribe exactly how many you should have in your arsenal, but start a collection of those which you can do well and continue to build your repertoire.

But even if you're great at learning accents and have a whole host of them in your back pocket, there will still be times when your accent for a character simply won't be spot on. For example, if a character was born in France, moved to the United States when they were five years old, and then emigrated to Belarus after college to live out their days, that would be one tough accent to master. And nobody would expect you to. Find an approximation for the accent and voice which blends together everything you know about that character and then keep it consistent. The listener's imagination will do the rest.

Vocal Attributes and Attitudes

Another method of creating characters for audiobooks is working with different vocal attributes and attitudes. For instance, two characters might be from the same place and may have even grown up together, but if one has a husky, low-pitched voice and the other a reedy, high-pitched voice, they're going to sound very different. This is a great start, but characters not only have to *sound* different; they have to *be* different and feel different to the listener. You need to fold in the many layers of who they are in the story: their past, their struggles, their hopes, and what drives them.

Of course, there is so much more to creating original character voices from scratch, which we can't go into without extending this work too far beyond its scope. If a project comes along which requires you to create and perform fully developed characters, some additional training might be useful.

Notation

How you prepare and notate your audiobooks is a matter of personal preference. Over time (and just by doing) you'll figure out what kind of notation you need to do in order to narrate well.

Audiobook narrator, Ana Clements, has graciously shared part of her process:

1. Read the book once through, underlining character descriptions and highlighting any attributions.*
2. Keep a separate sheet for character notes. During the read-through, note down everything that's available about each character—their age, what they do, significant life events, and the things which other characters think and say about them.

*When a character speaks in a book, their words generally appear before any indication of how they said them. For example, "Hey, hand me that spatula over there, would you please?" she shouted, in a mocking tone. You'll be well into the line before you realize what you needed to do with it, so highlighting these during your prep is a really good idea.

5 Performance

Written words on their own are lifeless things—mere splashes of ink on paper or blips on a screen. Until they're considered by a reader or brought to life through voice, they simply lie there, waiting to be interpreted and expressed. As Maya Angelou once wrote: "Words mean more than what is set down on paper. It takes the human voice to infuse them with shades of deeper meaning."[1] This chapter will show you how to do just that—infuse your narration reads with deeper meaning using your mind, body, voice, and your newly acquired tools.

I'd like to begin this section on performance with two nuggets of voiceover wisdom. The first of these appeared at the end of Chapter 1, but it bears repeating:

> The primary question we should ask ourselves as speakers is not "How can I manipulate my voice to sound like I imagine it should?" but rather "How can I manage the energy, intention, and emotion which will then *inform* and *influence* the sound of my voice?"

Understanding this distinction and putting it into practice will make a world of difference in the quality of your spoken word performances. It's something of a trade secret that will keep you on track while you're narrating and truly set your work apart.

The second has to do with our overall mindset as narrators:

> A spoken word performance is only as good as the speaker's state of mind. Mental clarity allows for expression without distraction and awareness without scrutiny.

This is why setting your foundations before you begin narrating is so important. If you pre-establish your framework and clear away the mental clutter, you'll be free to convey the client's message or tell the story, unencumbered by extraneous thought and judgment. In other words, you'll be in full flow during your performance.

In the opening chapter, I described the experience of being in this state while narrating or delivering a speech. It's worth revisiting here:

> *Any extraneous thoughts quickly fade away, your focus narrows to the task at hand, and you almost feel as though you've stepped into an alternate reality. You cannot say precisely how it's happening, but you are effortlessly transforming the text on the page into a coherent and connected performance. The words seem to go from your eyes to your body and voice with only a whisper of input from your mind. Even when you make a mistake, you are not distracted; you simply stop for a split second, pick up the last line, and continue as if it never happened. This is what it feels like to be in full flow as a speaker—to transcend the analytical mind and reach a place of pure expression.*

As much as I would love to give you a precise formula for achieving this state, I can only point the way and encourage you to practice and pay attention until it happens for you. Artistic performance of any kind is personal, nuanced, and highly resistant to a set of "fold tab A into slot B" instructions. Instead, I invite you to think of the following pages as a collection of performance-enhancing strategies—a menu of clues to help you reach that state of narration nirvana.

You may find all of them appealing or perhaps just a select few, and that's fine. The goal here is to help you improve your narration skills and connect more fully with your audience, so take whatever serves that purpose for you and leave the rest. Who knows—you may find that whatever you set aside now becomes more relevant to you down the road. Let's get started with the first order of business, which is getting yourself centered.

Alignment and Focus

We can't really perform any task well unless we're in the right frame of mind. In order to produce a great spoken word performance without many stumbles, we need to be fully calibrated and firmly rooted in performance mode.

Calibration

For many years now, I've used the word "calibrate" in my work with students. Merriam-Webster defines this word as "to adjust precisely for a particular function."[2] I use it when I talk about aligning one's inner experience with a performance outcome. In other words, we have to narrow any gap between what we believe we're conveying and what is actually captured on a recording and/or received by the listener.

For example, students new to voiceover often report that their performance of a character voice or narration text felt highly exaggerated while they were delivering it, only to learn that it actually came across as understated or even flat. This is a very common issue and the only remedy I've found is repetition—recording and listening back until you can accurately predict the results, based on what the performance *felt* like in your MBV. That's when you'll know that you're fully calibrated and in control of your skills.

Voice actors aren't the only creatives who refine their craft by aligning internal experience with external results. Dancers are a great example—they use mirrors as visual feedback to check that what they're experiencing in the body is creating the desired lines and fluidity of movement. Sculptors and painters also use visual cues, as they synchronize form, color, and composition with what they wish to express.

But here's the surprising thing: when we're fully immersed in pure creative flow, we don't concentrate on the physical component that's involved in the creating. For instance, a dancer doesn't think about their body, a sculptor doesn't think about their hands, and a voice actor doesn't think about their voice. The focus is placed *beyond* the apparatus—on the expression itself—and the body, hands, and voice are merely instruments of that expression. As an actor (voice or otherwise) the moment your attention turns inward to yourself and how you're coming across, you've stepped out of the flow and away from communicating with your audience.

Switching to Performance Mode

As mentioned before, most of your script prep will be done from your analytical side. You have to examine, consider, translate, research, decide, notate, and so on. But now that you're heading into the performance phase, you need to place your full trust in that prep and let it go. You now want to be operating primarily from your creative side, relying on intuition and your instincts with only a little input from the mind. Having done what you needed to do analytically, it's now time to step into the flow—to connect with yourself and your audience.

For some people, analyzing everything is a deeply ingrained habit and switching to performance mode isn't always so easy. The best bridges to help you cross over are visualization and emotion, but sometimes all it takes is a simple shift in perception.

Perception—Victor's Story

Victor was a new student and had booked an online coaching session. His initial reads were detached, impersonal, and seemed to be formulated to follow a certain cadence and melody. As an experienced audio engineer, this was how he approached his work—completely focused on getting the final result to sound a certain way. He also seemed to be firmly rooted in his left brain, with an impulse to analyze everything and methodically plot out his reads. The concept of creating an authentic performance from the inside out seemed alien to him.

We discussed the foundations for a short while, including right/ left brain, intention, speaking intuitively, and so on. He slowly began to release his need to analyze and control, and his reads became increasingly more authentic and believable. He then revealed that he was an experienced musician and had played the saxophone for many years. He told me how he could always hear the difference in his music when he was *thinking* about what he was playing as opposed to simply *expressing* himself through the instrument. It was a huge lightbulb moment for him (and a welcome real-world example for me). Now, he'll be able to rely on his own experience of playing music "unconsciously" and transfer that wisdom to his voiceover performances.

Incorporating The 7 Wavelengths

You may recall The 7 Wavelengths of Communication from Chapter 1 (one of the primary systems we need to keep in balance): perspective, body, language, emotion, voice, mind, and intuition. While I don't suggest that you think about these elements while you're in the middle of a read, it's a good idea to review them from time to time as part of your prep. Commit to integrating them into every performance and before long, keeping all seven in balance will become second nature.

The wavelengths can also be useful if you've been struggling with a read. Whatever the issue (and we're going to be looking at lots of common ones in the next chapter) consider where the imbalance may be coming from. Personally, I've found that just pinpointing the trouble spot can be enough to resolve it. For example, recognizing when my body isn't as involved as it should be, if I'm too focused on the words, or if my mind is getting in the way, snaps me back into the flow without having to do much. With practice, you'll learn to diagnose what's tripping you up and quickly make adjustments.

Translating "Client Speak"

While you probably won't be discussing your deepest narrator secrets with clients, you'll still need to have conversations with them about the project on which you're collaborating and understand what it is they need from your performance. Sometimes, you may have to practice your "translation" skills— taking the direction you're given and reinterpreting it into something which will actually alter the "DNA" of your read and not just the outer layer. Let me give you an example:

I was hired to do a voiceover for a book trailer. The copy arrived via email and I was surprised to find directions next to each and every line about how the voiceover should sound ("enumerative," "normal," "deeper," "theatrical," "sped up"). There were notes about which words should be emphasized and even when to take a deep breath for dramatic effect. When voice direction is this prescriptive, it's a sure sign that the writer has heard the finished performance in their head and is trying to describe this to the voice actor so they can duplicate it. This is really not the best way to work.

The chances that a narrator will spontaneously produce the precise read that someone has imagined are slim to none, so the stage is already set for disappointment. More importantly, if a voice actor strictly adhered to this type of step-by-step instruction, the resulting performance would feel mechanical and calculated. It would be the voiceover equivalent of painting by numbers. The finished product may resemble what it's meant to, but it would be fairly lifeless.

Back to my challenging client (who was actually a very nice person). In order to work with the script and deliver what he wanted, I had to tear down the notion of what the finished performance should sound like and rebuild it from the ground up. The first thing I did was copy the text and strip away all of his notes (temporarily). Then, I set my foundations:

Who am I?	Impartial narrator with an impish sense of humor
Who am I talking to?	Readers of young adult fiction
Intention	Entice, intrigue
Pace	6, moving to 7 in places (quite fast)
Formality	3–4 (very informal)
Visuals	Animation
Emotional set-point	Fun, teasing

I read it aloud a couple of times until it felt right, then referred back to the client's notes to check that everything he had envisioned had been organically baked into the read. Success! If I had tried to deliver each line according to the very specific voice direction, the result would have been an incoherent mess—pure vocal manipulation and mental analysis rather than a grounded, connected performance. But that's the job— putting the project pieces together (completely dismantling them first, if necessary) then delivering a quality performance that connects with the audience.

Naturally, my client wanted the voiceover for his project to be performed well and to sound "right," and did his best to convey what he wanted from the read. In all probability, he thought he was being helpful and thorough in providing such specific direction. But as he's not a narrator himself, he had difficulty articulating what he wanted in "narrator speak," so it was my job to translate it.

This is our superpower as voice actors and narrators—taking whatever text, information, and direction is provided and transforming it into a performance that's even better than expected. It's our responsibility to use our gifts and skills to interpret the client's vision, internalize it, feed it into our narration machinery, and then communicate it with clarity.

Let's Get Physical (and Emotional)

Gesturing

Many years ago, I had issues with my adrenal glands. Most of the time I was in "fight or flight," which meant that every aspect of my life felt urgent and rushed. This seriously affected my narration reads and clients often had to ask me to slow down. That's when I discovered the true power of gesturing.

When you use your hands while narrating, you're not only engaging the body in order to enhance the read, but you're also setting the tempo for yourself. Movement helps you "conduct" your performance, so if your body sets the pace, your speech will naturally follow.

Voice acting doesn't just happen from the neck up. Like any other kind of acting, the whole body needs to be involved. And although you can't leave the microphone to walk around, even just jiggling a foot or doing some subtle hand gesturing will be enough to bring your body into the mix and lift the read. The gestures don't even need to be related to what you're saying.

I once worked on a technical project for engineers where I had to describe complex machinery and explain how one subsystem fits together with another. My hands were all over the place while I described how this "whirligig" was coupled with that "doodad." The movements made no real sense, but without them, the reads would have been flat as a pancake and very dull indeed.

Emotion

Without emotional investment, voiceover performances can be reduced to merely pleasant voices reading aloud. Part of our job as narrators is to find a way into the feeling of what we're saying. For example, a corporate narration about how proud a company is of its employees' achievements must be infused with a genuine sense of pride or the audience simply won't feel it. If you can't quite generate this from your position of company representative, then you'll have to find another way in.

If you're more of a visual person, recall an event when you were filled with pride, and picture every detail. If you're kinesthetic, get some excitement in your body before the read by flapping your hands, jumping up and down, or grinning from ear to ear. If you're auditory, practice emoting aloud or maybe listen to something which makes you feel a sense of pride. Do whatever you need to in order to get yourself fizzing with the feeling of what you're saying. If music is part of the project, always ask to hear it or, better yet, have it in your ears while you're delivering the read. It's the quickest way I know of to connect emotionally with the copy.

Breathing

We breathe in and out all day, every day, and most of the time we don't give it a second thought. We count on our breath to carry on in the background, whether we're aware of it or not. When we're having a conversation with someone, we don't plan when we're going to take a breath or wonder how much more we'll be able to say before needing a top-up. It all happens naturally. So, why is breathing such a problem area for us voice actors? You may already be familiar with some of the classic issues around breathing:

1. Running out of air before the end of a sentence or phrase.
2. Becoming self-conscious about noisy breathing.
3. Worrying about where to breathe in a long sentence.

Paradoxically, most breathing issues tend to vanish when you stop thinking about them. When you're completely focused on communicating and connecting with the listener, your breathing tends to become instinctive.

Of course, you will occasionally come across a beast of a script that challenges this theory and forces you to actually plan where you might be able to get some air. Medical and technical scripts are just such animals. It's not uncommon for this type of copy to be lifted straight from a textbook or technical manual, and not written especially for the spoken word. You could be faced with an entire paragraph comprised of one long sentence. In these cases (if altering the script is not possible) it may well be necessary to make a note of where you intend to breathe. Marking breaths in a script is not ideal for all the reasons covered throughout this book, but unless you can negotiate a script change with the client, you might just have to grin and bear it. And then breathe.

Managing Nervous Energy

Our society calls it anxiety; Buddhists call it "monkey mind." It's that state when your heart and adrenal glands are pumping like crazy and your mind is darting between regrets about the past, fears about the future, and worries about controlling the present. Needless to say, it's very difficult to do anything well in the midst of such chaos, let alone be relaxed, focused, and creative in front of a microphone.

In the early days, I would get so nervous before a session that it was almost debilitating, so I get it. Eventually, I learned and developed strategies to quiet my little monkey (or at least keep her occupied) in order to get the job done. I'm going to share what I've learned but, before I do, let's look at what we're dealing with.

Adrenaline versus Nerves

Picture the scene: You're in a studio behind a glass panel with several tense-looking people on the other side, plus an engineer. Each one has a slightly different idea about how to approach this recording session and they all demand to feel pleased by the end of it. You would have to be superhuman if your adrenaline wasn't pumping just a tad.

Biologically speaking, your body can't tell the difference between an adrenaline rush about something positive and nervousness about something negative.[3] But notice what happens when you say each of these sentences aloud: "I am excited" and "I am nervous." Did you detect a subtle difference? It may only be a matter of perception, but keep this distinction in mind the next time you step into a performance or audition situation. Acknowledging excitement rather than nerves will help you feel more positive and you'll be better able to channel that surge of energy and use it to your advantage.

A little adrenaline can be a good thing for performers. Some (including myself) even see it as a necessity. On those occasions when my adrenaline was very low or even absent, my performance suffered. I need that extra jolt to sharpen my mind and get the juices flowing. But if adrenaline gets out of control, that's another thing altogether. If too much of this hormone floods your system, you could stray into the territory of a panic attack, and I can tell you from personal experience that this will *not* be a state you can use to your advantage. Allow me to share a painful episode that illustrates this very clearly.

Many years ago, I was invited to attend an audition for an animated series, which was being produced by a very well-known company (whose mascot is a rodent in red shorts). I was both terrified and excited, but mostly terrified. In the days that preceded my meeting with the casting director, I had whipped myself into a frenzy with unbridled thoughts like "This is it—my big break!" or "Everything is riding on this!" and probably one or two darker thoughts such as "If I don't get this job, my career is over!" Spoiler alert—the audition did not go well.

By the time I arrived at the casting, I was in a full-blown state of anxiety and I knew from bitter experience that one of two survival mechanisms would kick in at any moment: my mind would either choose to shut down completely or it would go into overdrive, causing a torrent of verbal diarrhea. I entered the room, offered a sweaty palm to the nice young lady and felt that choice involuntarily arising within me. Right—verbal diarrhea it is.

The next few minutes were an unconscious, babbling blur of me listing virtues, demonstrating all the "voices" I could do, and pleadings of the "you-really-need-me-for-this-job" variety. When I finally paused for breath and she was able to get a word in, she asked a follow-up question about a skill I'd proudly claimed to have (accents, I think it was). That's when my mind flipped the switch to shut-down mode. I couldn't remember my own name, let alone my native Colorado accent, or any other accent I might be able to do. I must have muttered something in reply, but I can't be certain. I have no recollection of thanking her for her time or saying goodbye. So, when I say "I get it," I really do.

Let's look at those strategies I mentioned to help you manage your energy (nervous or otherwise) during a session or audition and keep your monkey mind in check.

Breathe

When we feel threatened or stressed, the rhythm of our breathing changes, which upsets oxygen levels, which in turn can affect brain function.[4] If you can, sit for five minutes before a performance or audition and regulate your breathing. Slowly count to four on the inhale, and eight on the exhale. A longer exhale stimulates the vagal nerve, bringing the body into "rest-and-digest" and away from "fight-or-flight."[5]

You can repeat this process during a session when the committee on the other side of the glass is discussing the read you just did. Whatever you do, try not to let your imagination run wild about what they're thinking or what their facial expressions might mean. They could just be trying to decide what to order for lunch.

Lower the Stakes

Of course you want to deliver an excellent performance, who doesn't? But there are no lives on the line if you get it slightly wrong. You need to find a way to care about the job you're there to do, without imagining dire consequences if it doesn't go exactly to plan. Sometimes, when I'm super nervous (sorry, *excited*) about an upcoming session, I imagine what I'm going to do the day *after*. This is calming because it reminds me that, when it's over, life will go on.

Status

You are a chosen member of the team which has been assembled to complete this project for the end client (who may or may not be in the room). You are no more or less important than anyone else. Of course, there are still protocols to adhere to during a session (more about this in Chapter 8) but as far as status is concerned, you are all there to work together and get the job done.

Staying in the Flow

You can probably remember a time when you experienced an easy flow while speaking and felt that you were very articulate. Maybe you were having a heart-to-heart with someone close to you, or you were addressing a group of people on a subject you feel passionate about. What do you suppose was happening (or not happening) during those times that made your message so clear?

For me, I am most articulate when speaking from the heart and not the head. At those times, my analytical mind is not engaged and I'm not distracted by thoughts about how I'm sounding, what my hair looks like, or what I need to get at the grocery store later on. I am fully present, in the zone, expressing myself, and connecting with whoever I'm talking to. This is the key to being a great narrator—staying in the flow as often as you can and finding your way back in when you falter. It sounds so simple, doesn't it?

Unfortunately, I can guarantee you that there will be times when you will not be in the zone. In fact, sometimes you will be so far out of the zone that you won't even know where the zone is. Don't worry—this happens to all of us. The secret is learning to recognize your personal patterns:

1. When you've stepped out.
2. Why you've stepped out.
3. How to get yourself back in quickly with minimal fuss.

An obvious outward sign of being out of the zone is frequent stumbling. If you're making lots of mistakes and can't readily identify the cause (such as a script error or a pronunciation problem), you will usually find that it's an inner management issue and you'll need to ask yourself some questions in order to diagnose the problem:

1. Is there mental interference such as distraction, judgment, or worry?
2. Is my focus wandering from expression to self-monitoring?
3. Am I trying to control the read or working too hard to make it sound "just so"?

Once you understand how your mind-body-voice team operates and how to manage it, the next step is to develop strategies for getting yourself back on track after you've been derailed. I can provide some pointers, but your remedies will be very specific to you.

Personally, when I'm struggling and making lots of mistakes, it's usually because I'm listening to myself or trying to think my way through the read, rather than feel my way through. I can usually resolve the issue by:

1. Revisiting the foundations.
2. Reminding myself of who I'm talking to and why.
3. Reconnecting physically and emotionally.

With practice, you'll discover what usually knocks you out of the flow and what you need to do to jump back in. It may be that you simply need to take a deep breath to recenter yourself, stretch and shake it out, take a bathroom break, or (if you're recording alone) walk away for half an hour and clear your head. Getting to know your individual performance quirks (and we all have them) means you'll have remedies standing by when things get dicey (which they will from time to time). The bottom line is this:

> Flow is always available to us—the trick is to keep ourselves from putting a kink in the hose.

Silencing the Inner Critic

We'll finish this chapter by taking a look at the dreaded inner critic. We all have one. Some performers have learned to tame theirs; others are constantly plagued by a negative commentator who perches on their shoulder (that's where mine sits, anyway) and whispers in their ear that whatever they're trying to create is simply not good enough.

Perhaps you're like me and have one of those insistent inner critics. I realized long ago that it's no good trying to override the little monster and try to convince it that you do actually know what you're doing. Because here's what I've learned: when that little voice is active, it's because you *do* have doubts. Your inner critic is only echoing the self-limiting beliefs that you already possess. And until your confidence and self-belief grow strong enough to relegate your critic to the outer fringes of your life, you need to find a way to reconcile with it and come to an understanding.

The Brat

Perhaps because I'm a character actor at heart, my critic has been well and truly personified. She is a five-year-old, red-haired brat with braids and freckles (probably created out of images of "Pippi Longstocking" from my youth) and she used to be quite the little madam. We actually made friends a long time ago and agreed that, while I was performing, painting, knitting, or doing anything else creative, she would keep still and silent and then afterward, she could have her say. This may sound a little nuts, but it worked really well for a very long time. I don't know exactly when she left or where she went, but I haven't had any run-ins with her for quite some time. Perhaps she realized that she could no longer push my buttons and just grew tired of trying.

Now, I wouldn't dream of suggesting that you turn your own inner critic into a character you then have conversations with, but do try to find a lighthearted way to manage that little voice in your head if it whispers to you that you're not good enough. You are good enough. Once more with feeling—*you are good enough*. Unfortunately, no one else has the power to tell you this and have it get through to you—you've simply got to realize it for yourself.

6 Pitfalls

I've made a ton of mistakes in my career, some so subtle that no one would have noticed and others so glaringly obvious that the memory of them still makes me shudder a little. But through all the missteps, I've discovered what works, what doesn't, and why.

Decades of trial, error, and observation have made me keenly aware of my own internal narrating machinery. I can sense what it feels like when I'm delivering a strong read, what's in the way when I'm struggling, and how to make adjustments to get myself back on track.

I have also learned a great deal from working with other voice actors. By asking probing questions when a read wasn't going so well and noting their overall mindset, perception, or visualization, certain performance issues emerged which seem to be universal.

This chapter will help you to identify and navigate some of the most common of these pitfalls, which may be standing between you and a great narration read. I know them intimately, because I've lived them and seen so many other narrators struggle with them as well.

An opportunity to learn from someone else's mistakes is incredibly valuable, whether you're learning a new skill, supplementing those you already have, or just brushing up. It's the least painful way to gather knowledge and can save you a whole lot of time, energy, and embarrassment. When you're not the one in the hot seat, the stakes (and adrenaline) are considerably lower.

Of course you will still make blunders of your own, but you may as well give yourself a head start by learning from those who have gone before you. Let's begin with the most common issue of them all.

Out of Focus

Issues around focus are probably the biggest obstacles to a great narration read. I've experienced them myself countless times (and still do) and have seen them trip up students more often than anything else. Most of the time, it's not so much that we have a *lack* of focus—it's just pointed in the wrong direction.

The most common problem seems to be thinking about the read itself and how to "get it right," but any type of distraction will pull us out of the zone. When we become unfocused as speakers, our message becomes unfocused too, and that forces our audience to work overtime.

At one time or another, you've probably been to a talk or lecture when you just couldn't keep your eyes open. Maybe it was because you weren't interested in the topic or you'd been out too late the night before, but it might have been that the speaker wasn't communicating *with* you, they were talking *at* you (while possibly thinking about where to grab dinner afterward).

As narrators, when we get distracted—even if it's by thoughts about what we're narrating—our energy gets diffused and the listener will have to work extra hard to follow us and take in what we're saying. Imagine them having to mentally run around, collecting all the shattered pieces of our message, and trying to glue them together *while* they're listening to us! We never want to make our audience work that hard. If we are focused and connected, our listeners will be too.

So, how do you keep yourself sharp during a voiceover performance? As we've discussed at length, getting yourself aligned before the read is half the battle. As for staying on track while you're in the thick of it, the simple answer is—be present. I realize this is sometimes easier said than done, so here are some basic tips:

1. Feel your way through a read rather than think your way through.
2. Engage your body with gestures and facial expressions.
3. Engage your intuitive right brain with visualization.

I can pretty much guarantee that you'll encounter focus issues from time to time. The trick is to recognize them and bring yourself back to center, without letting your monkey mind beat you up about it.

Perfectionism—The Toxic Read Killer

As the owner/operator of an OCD-prone brain, I understand all too well the urge to perfect everything, but if you allow this impulse to have free reign over your performances, it can become a real problem.

I confess that I'm a bit partial to feeling in control and just love for my work to be "perfect." But here's what I've learned: the more you try to shape, bend, or otherwise force your performance into sounding "just so," the more it will unravel. There have been many times when I was certain I'd tweaked a narration read to perfection during the recording and then again in the edit (you know, just to be sure) only to discover that I had unwittingly sterilized the life out of it. By focusing solely on the audible outcome, the heart and soul of the communication were lost.

When we're stuck in perfecting mode, our foundations become unstable—we lose sight of who we're talking to and why. Our carefully chosen intention for the read shifts to "Do this right!" or the even more precarious "Don't mess up!" Try to imagine another person standing over you and shouting these things while you're trying to work. Would you put up with that, even for a second? Yet this is what we do to ourselves, while somehow expecting a perfect performance to come out of it.

Perfectionism is about control and it's a permanent resident of the left brain, which wants everything (and everyone) to be orderly, categorized, and predictable. The urge to perfect everything is actually driven by anxiety and fear, which will knock you out of the flow every time. Here are some antidotes:

1. Focus on what you're saying, to whom, and why, rather than how you sound or how your performance might be perceived.

2. Loosen your grip on the notion of perfection. There's actually no such thing—there is only perception. The tighter you hold on, the more wooden your performance will become.

3. Don't nail down your performance so tightly that the message can't breathe. Give your audience time to consider what you're saying.

Looping Syndrome (or the Self-Conscious Read)

Speak. Listen. Judge. Repeat. This is the sticky mental loop of the self-conscious read, or "looping syndrome" as I call it. This sneaky beast tripped me up for years, but once I figured out how it was interfering with my reads, I was able to escape the merry-go-round once and for all. You may find the stages of this circular trap all too familiar. This is how it usually goes:

1. You begin reading.

2. Start monitoring yourself.

3. Judge what you're hearing.

4. Change what you're doing.

5. Loop back around again.

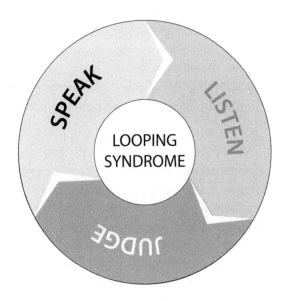

Figure 3 Looping Syndrome.

Imagine trying to produce a great narration read with this swirling mental commotion going on in the background. And the cycle spins around so quickly that you may not even be aware that it's happening. But there are clear warning signs when you're caught in this nightmarish loop-de-loop and headed for trouble.

Apart from feeling awkward and self-conscious, you may notice that the read doesn't seem to be flowing all that well and it feels like very hard work. You'll probably also be making lots of mistakes. And why shouldn't you be—you're attempting to deliver a crystal-clear message while hacking your way through a tornado of cognitive debris. It would be a miracle if you were in this state and not stumbling all over the place!

The Self-Conscious Trap

If you've ever sat across from a mirror in a meeting room or taken part in a video conference, you'll understand how seeing yourself while you're speaking can make you feel uncomfortable and self-conscious. You have to work extra hard to express yourself and stay on message without being thrown off by your own image looking back at you. It doesn't matter if you're pleased with what you see or find it abhorrent—it can still be off-putting.

When the 2020 pandemic hit, workshops and coaching sessions had to be conducted online, which was something I had always largely avoided due to the cringe factor of seeing myself while I was teaching. But I was surprised at how quickly I became accustomed to it. With enough exposure, it ceased being a distraction. It's the same with any kind of voiceover performance—with enough practice and experience, you'll stop being self-conscious about the sound of your own voice (or your thoughts about what you're doing with it), and you'll be able to focus on just getting the job done.

Exiting the Roundabout

So how do you break out of looping syndrome? How do you resist being pulled into this negatively charged vortex? To answer these questions, let's refer back to the narrator archetypes described in Chapter 2.

The archetypes which are most likely to have an issue with looping syndrome are The Worrier, The Perfectionist, and The Monitor. If the symptoms of the self-conscious read seem familiar to you, you might have identified with one or more of these. Here's a reminder of the keys to overcoming the negative aspects of these archetypes, which can also help you break out of looping syndrome:

The Worrier—Confidence

The Perfectionist—Letting Go

The Monitor—Focus

If you're still having difficulty stopping the cycle of listening to and judging yourself during a read, you may need to resort to a little trickery in the short term. Try one of the following with your headphones:

1. Turn down the levels.
2. Have one side on and one off.
3. Go without headphones altogether.

When you hear yourself more naturally, it can help you feel less self-conscious. You can then slowly work your way back up to full volume and having your headphones on both ears.

Hyper-Aural

A cousin of the self-conscious read is something I call "hyper-aural" which simply means overly focused on your sense of hearing. If you find yourself paying too much attention to every little sound you're making, that's going to be distracting. Let's look at what happens when you get into this state and how you can get yourself out of it.

The first thing that happens is that you lose sight of who you're talking to and why, and then your ears go into overdrive. You begin to notice even the tiniest mouth noise, the sound of your own heartbeat, or whether your tongue fully connected with your palate on that "t" word. Then, you really enter the spin cycle: the more you notice, the more offtrack you get; the more offtrack you get, the worse your read becomes; the worse you read becomes, the more you notice what's wrong with your read. Round and round you go in a self-perpetuating spiral and before long, you're in the audio version of a house of mirrors where everything seems distorted and amplified.

Here's how you get out: get out. Take a break and if you can, leave the booth for a few minutes. Even the toughest of clients can't argue with you needing a bathroom break. Recenter yourself and let go of the perfectionist mindset that got you into trouble in the first place. Refresh your foundations, take a few deep breaths, and go back in.

Bad Habits and How to Break Them

Habits, by their very nature, are unconscious. We repeat an action over and over again until it becomes so automatic that we don't even realize we're doing it. If we want to change an unwanted habit, we need three things: awareness, effort, and repetition.

Sometimes, only the first of these is necessary. Bad narration habits can often be remedied just by becoming aware of them. For example, when I point out to a student that before every breath, they make a lip-smacking sound, that's usually all it takes to sort it out. Once they're aware of it, the issue vanishes. Other times, a bad habit is dug in like a tick, so a little effort and repetition is needed to extract it and send it on its way.

Fading Phrase Ends

This is a very common issue and one that I encounter quite often when working with students of all levels. It's when you run out of steam at the ends of phrases or sentences. Here are the three primary causes, along with suggested remedies:

1. Impatience

   You're eager to move on to the next section in the copy, so you don't quite finish what you're doing with the current one.

   Work on being present during the read. Stay focused on your place in the text, the foundations that you've set, and enjoying your time at the mic.

2. Need for Control

   While you're finishing one sentence or phrase, you're looking ahead to work out what to do with the next.

   Presence is the answer here too, along with trust. If you've prepped well for the read, trust that, and shift your focus to expression, rather than trying to control the read.

3. Running Out of Breath

   The third cause is running out of breath. We covered this in some detail in the last chapter, but what I will say here is that poor breathing habits are very common (and something I struggled with in the beginning). Here's what I've learned:

   - Keep your lungs topped up.
   - Stop thinking so much about your breathing.

Snatching Breaths and Smacking

While it's obviously a good idea for you to breathe while you're narrating, making lots of noise while you do it is not. Sharp, loud intakes of air and lip-smacking sounds on the in breath are the bane of a sound engineer's life. And part of your job as a narrator is to make the engineer's job as easy as possible, whether that role is being filled by someone else or yourself.

One remedy for these habits is just becoming aware of them. Record yourself when you work with practice scripts and listen out for unnecessary breathing noise. Of course, the best way to eradicate them is to edit your own recordings. After the umpteenth time lifting out a lip smack or loud gulp of air, or having to do a retake because your breathing crashed into your speech, I guarantee that you'll change your ways.

Reading Too Far Ahead

This is another function of impatience or anxiety. You're reading and planning too far ahead, which causes you to gloss over words or stumble.

The remedies (yet again) are presence and trust. Slow down, stay where you are in the copy, and trust that you'll instinctively know what to do when the next sentence arrives. I love the analogy of driving on a winding road in the fog so I'll say it again: if you start planning how you're going to handle three curves ahead, you are sure to crash.

The Self-Imposed Error Quota

Whether I'm working with a client in a studio or recording from home, I sometimes have an internal alarm bell that screams at me that I've reached my limit of mistakes—"That's it, girl! You have arrived at your error quota. One more stumble and you're out!" It's an illusion, of course, and probably the love child of my inner critic and my perfectionism. Insecurity can add so much unnecessary pressure to us and our performances. Let me share a cautionary tale.

I was recording an audiobook and working with a producer remotely. I was plagued by the notion that I was making far more mistakes than any other audiobook narrator in history and, as he was in another part of the country, I couldn't read his body language or facial expressions to gauge how he was feeling about it. On about day three of recording, I decided to air my concerns. Was I making more mistakes than other people he'd worked with? He surprised me with actual statistics that completely put my mind at rest—I was doing fine. Not only did I wish that I'd asked my question on day one, but also that I hadn't spent all that time and energy worrying at all.

Here's what I learned: there *is* no error quota, above which you will be branded a bad narrator. That's not to say that you're free to do a poor job, just don't beat yourself up for making mistakes and being like every other narrator on the planet—human. It's a universal law that the more energy you put into worrying about something, the nearer you bring it toward you. Simply do your best, handle any errors with grace, refocus, and then keep going.

Fluffing with Grace

Early Warning System

Before we talk about the best ways to handle mistakes when they occur, you need to understand and manage how they come to your attention in the first place. Major stumbles or missing words will be obvious, so you'll know about those instantly. But what about the more subtle errors, such as a popping "p," a clarity issue, or a noisy page turn? You want to be aware that these things have happened, but from a distance, so you're not taken out of the performance.

For all the reasons outlined in previous chapters, the last thing you want to do during a narration read is to monitor yourself. You cannot remain focused on your performance if you're also listening out for mistakes. So what do you do? The simple answer is: you learn to sense it.

With practice, you'll cultivate an awareness that operates in the background, which lets you know when you've made a mistake or when a retake is needed, but which doesn't completely derail your read. Please note that this is *not* a job for your inner critic, unless they're tame enough to just give you a heads-up without any extraneous commentary.

Do not ignore the signal that you've fluffed. If you disregard it and try to keep barreling through, it will stick in your narration machinery like a paper jam and then you'll be more likely to make an even bigger mistake. It's easier to just retake the line and then you can carry on, undistracted.

Conditioned Fluff Response

When you make a mistake, train yourself to become nonreactive—no apology, no grunt, no slapping your thigh—just start the sentence again and keep going.

Behind every fluff reaction (whether it's vocal, physical, or just an internal reprimand) there's a collection of negative thoughts that whiz through your mind so quickly that you may not even be aware of them: "Damn! Another mistake!" "What's wrong with me today? I know better than that!" How in the world can you expect to narrate well with chatter like that going on in the background?

Practice stopping and starting without reaction—first externally and then internally—until having a stumble feels every bit as natural as a read that's on rails. The only indication to the engineer that you've made an error should be repeated text. Do not force them to edit out you verbally flogging yourself, making excuses, or apologizing all over the place.

Too Many Hats

In the current landscape (especially since the pandemic) everyone and their cat has a home studio, which means that we have to act as narrator, producer, and sound engineer. For your own sanity, I suggest that you keep these roles as separate as possible.

After you've done your prep, put on your voice actor hat (obviously a beret, set at a rakish angle) and just do that job. Then, you can switch to your producer's hat (fedora) for the playback; back to voice actor for any pick-ups; to your sound engineer's beanie for the editing; and, finally, back to the producer to wrap up the job. I've tried wearing all the hats at once and for me, it's not a good look and doesn't produce my best work.

Ghosts of the Past

It can be difficult to avoid bringing the habits of our past into the present. Training and experiences within other performance disciplines or even unrelated careers can become ingrained in our system and influence what we do as communicators.

As we learn to become better narrators, we need to be aware of how past experiences might be coloring our reads. The following are instances I've come across where the habits of previous experience had an effect on narration performance.

Airport Announcer

I once worked with a student who approached every piece of narration copy with a forceful, formal style. It was perplexing until he shared that he had worked at an international airport for many years making announcements. The vocal style he'd used for so long at this job had become a permanent part of his communication style and we had to work very hard to shake him free of it.

Commercial Voice Actor

Commercial voiceovers (especially radio) have a very different feel than most narration projects. Voice actors who have done a lot of commercial work usually have to overcome the inherent vocal intonations of "the sell." With practice, they can learn to let go of that read and step into a more authentic narration performance.

Lawyer

In Chapter 2, I shared the story of Trisha, whose manner became super formal and harsh the moment she stood up from her chair to walk to the microphone. She had been an English barrister for many years, and the act of standing to speak had become stubbornly linked to a specific vocal tone and formality. We started her off in a seated position and slowly changed her posture until the ghosts of her past had finally been laid to rest.

Music Teacher

I was working remotely with a student who had a habit of projecting far more than was needed for the copy we were working with. At first, I assumed it was because we were working online, but then learned that she had been a music teacher for many years. This made perfect sense to me. Teachers in general have to project, but music teachers often have to shout over the instruments to be heard. She had taken this habit of communication with her into her narration practice. Once she made the connection between her former job and her current style of narrating, the problem resolved itself.

On-Camera Presenter

A student in an online workshop gave her first read of some narration copy. As I listened with my eyes closed, I kept picturing her doing a piece to camera. There was something about the delivery—it was slightly projected, and I felt like she was doing more than she needed to physically. It turned out she did a lot of hosting work and it was really showing up in her reads. As soon as she shifted her foundations, identified who she was talking to, and set a clear intention, she was able to deliver a strong narration performance.

Theater Actor

Trained theater actors, or those who have done a lot of stage work, have a tendency to project. They are accustomed to performing in an environment where voice and physicality are amplified. These actors need to overcome their stage habits in favor of a new set of instincts for narration work. For them, the switch is similar to when they have to go from stage to screen acting. With practice, they can easily swap to what's required for narration work.

7 Practice

Becoming proficient in any skill takes training, repetition, observation, more repetition, and time. In this chapter, you'll have the opportunity to work with a wide variety of narration copy, while putting all of your new learning into practice.

Each sample script is followed by a few notes to guide you through any potential trouble spots (it would be beneficial for you to work through the pieces on your own before reading them). We'll look at things like mindset, visualization, and the foundational elements including positioning, visuals, intention, pace, and formality.

As you practice with the text, I encourage you to also work on being aware of and managing your inner processes. As we've learned, when you're out of balance or distracted, you'll make completely different choices because you'll be trying to manipulate the performance in some way, rather than letting it flow through you.

Also, I strongly suggest recording and listening back during your practice, as this is by far the quickest way to progress. You may recall the section on calibration in Chapter 5. The repetition of record and playback will serve to calibrate your performance—narrowing any gap between what you believe you're creating and what is actually being captured on the recording.

Audiobooks

Transferred by Dian Perry (Science Fiction)

Casey's body arched suddenly and jolted her awake as she gasped for air. She'd had the dream again—immersed in watery blackness, bubbles issuing from her nose and mouth, her long blond hair swirling around her head like an ancient sea creature. She experienced the all too familiar feeling of utter helplessness with arms and legs flailing, searching for purchase as she desperately tried to reach the surface and ease the unbearable burning in her lungs.

Back in the room, her face damp with sweat, and her breathing now beginning to slow, she fluttered open encrusted eyelids and could just make out a slowly rotating ceiling fan which she did not recognize. She was lying on a bed, that much she knew. It was not particularly uncomfortable, but her lower back reported that it was certainly not the high-tech, expensive memory foam that she and Darren had purchased together last spring. "Where *is* Darren?" she wondered vaguely, desperate to break through the debilitating mental fog to remember how she got here and where exactly "here" was.

Her mouth was bone dry and her lips felt swollen and cracked. She couldn't quite place it, but the taste of salted metal in her mouth was familiar somehow. Had she been drinking? She noted a slight headache but it was nothing like the hangovers of her youth. Now thirty years old, she had mellowed considerably, and meeting Darren two years earlier had brought her squarely into a more mature, responsible phase in her life. There had even been much joyful talk between them of having a child, which she'd never been certain about before meeting Darren. But watching him with his baby nieces and nephews had awakened something within her that she had never even realized was there.

Frowning, Casey rubbed her eyes with the back of her hand. She supposed it was early morning, but she couldn't be certain. Propping herself up on her elbows, she tried to bring the room into focus. It was tiny, dimly lit, and smelled faintly of bleach and rose-scented air freshener. The twin bed with its thin, gray airline-style blanket and coverless pillow was wedged into the corner along the outside wall and there was only a foot or so between the other two sides and the stark, yellowing walls. There was no visible door.

A small window to her right, its edges showing more wood than paint, framed a distant city skyline she had only seen in progress reports, the compiling of which was a large part of the job she detested on the Saturn outpost.

Notes

This is about as simple as audiobook narration gets—it is pure narrative storytelling. There are two bits of guidance I can offer here:

1. Keep the pace on the slower side to allow the visuals to develop in the listener's mind.

2. Don't put too much into the voice, which is an easy trap to fall into when there is drama or tension. Just make sure that you feel the intrigue and let that come through naturally, rather than forcing your voice to sound that way.

Your role is that of impartial narrator, and the audience is young adult. The overall intention might be to entertain, but it would be helpful to set an intention that's is a bit more refined and specific, such as "intrigue" or "mystify." You'll be reading to one person, so the overall feel will be quite intimate.

The text itself needs minimal prep. There are no character voices to create, and no obvious pronunciation issues to investigate. Notation isn't really necessary either as there are no over-long sentences that need breaking up or complex phrasing to mark.

Road Rage by Dian Perry (Mystery Fiction)

"Hand me that crescent wrench there on the cart, would ya?" said Lindy, from underneath the 1975 Pontiac Grand Prix. Her voice was even huskier than usual this morning. She'd been out late the night before at Josh's thirtieth birthday party, and must have had more to drink than she thought. When the bright dawn light had streamed through her bedroom window and woken her up, she'd had no memory of getting into bed or even coming home, for that matter. She felt like six kinds of hell and was grateful that she was lying down and hidden beneath her arctic blue Pontiac, which she adored.

To her left, she glimpsed an oily pair of blue canvas shoes and the tattered cuffs of grimy gray overalls as the requested silver tool appeared near her head. "Thanks," she said, grabbing it with a greasy hand and continuing her work on the car's undercarriage. Her head was pounding and it felt like her eyes were being pushed out of their sockets. She hadn't had a hangover for more than three months, but this one seemed to be making up for lost time. "Geez, you look like shit. How late did you stay last night?" called Danny, Lindy's business partner and the owner of the tattered overalls. He had just switched on the radio and tuned it to his favorite classic rock station. Lindy winced at the noise and replied in a louder voice than she wanted to, "Not late. Left just after you, I think."

It was a lie, of course. The truth was she had very little recollection of the evening and nothing at all about when she left or with whom. She remembered arriving at the bar with a birthday gift and a hug for her little brother; flashes of meeting and greeting a few of his friends whom she barely knew, and then a handsome waiter making the rounds with a tray of drinks and a dazzling smile. After that, it was all blank.

What surprised her most was that she had no memory of the big decision of whether or not to have a drink at all. All the official literature and everyone at her weekly meetings were always talking about "the moment" when you're forced to decide between having a good time for right now and choosing sobriety for a good life forever. Why couldn't she remember agonizing over that decision? She had been doing so well. Why would she suddenly blow it at her brother's lame birthday party?

She certainly wasn't looking forward to the awkward conversation with her sponsor—dealing with the shame of admitting that she had lost her day count. Three months sober down the pan. "Shit. *That's* gonna be fun," she grunted sarcastically under her breath, as she strained to loosen a stubborn nut on the chassis. Letting out a sigh and resting for a minute before tackling the next, she was grateful to be lying on her car creeper which was fitted with a soft leather headrest. "God, my head," she thought. She strained her head back and to the right, intending to ask Danny to turn down the music, which was blasting some 80s rock tune from the workbench across the garage. That's when she saw it.

There was something on the inside of the driver's side wheel well. At first, she thought it was just mud and grass, though she didn't remember driving through anything like that recently. Using the heels of her work boots and her left hand on the chilly concrete floor, she pushed the creeper over a few inches to get a better look. It wasn't mud *or* grass—it was blood. Blood and hair. Her body froze while she stared at it and her mind raced. How long has that been there? The blood had congealed slightly, but it certainly wasn't dried. The hair that was matted into the crimson paste didn't look like it had belonged to an animal.

A chill went up and down Lindy's spine. Her body went numb and all at once, she knew that there was so much more to the events of the previous night than she could even fathom.

Notes

This is a mystery novel, so let the suspense come through in your voice, without overdoing it. There are two character voices to create here. You've been given the information that Lindy's voice is naturally husky, but extra husky on this day. There isn't much information on Danny at this stage, but he's a mechanic and business owner who enjoys 1980s classic rock, so you could work with that to develop a voice for him. This excerpt contains a bit of dialogue, so you can ease into practicing the switch from character to narrator—give yourself a beat when going from one to the other.

Gordon's Heart by Dian Perry (Children's Fiction)

This is Gordon. And that red pillow-like thing tucked under his arm is Gordon's heart. Years ago, when the little black gorilla was first put together at the factory, the small stuffed heart was sewn between his paws and onto his black furry chest. But after a while, he found that he just couldn't express himself as he wanted to. So he let his unstuffed friend, Arletta, carefully separate it. His paws and arms would then be free for all kinds of fun things like waving, bowing, and his favorite thing of all—hugging! Although he chose to have it separated, Gordon's heart is still very special to him.

One day, Dilbert O'Sullivan (a gray, speckled primate, and a recent arrival at Primrose Hall) asked Gordon about his heart. "Why is it so important to you?" Gordon replied in his patient and wise way, "Well, it is a part of me. It has been with me since the day I was sewn. And even though we are no longer connected physically, it is still full of the same stuff that makes up me—my energy. Do you understand?" Dilbert paused for a minute, staring at the heart, trying to take in what Gordon had said. He suddenly had an idea and his eyes lit up with excitement. "Can I look after it for you when you go away tomorrow?"

Gordon was planning an overnight trip with his unstuffed pal, Brian, and would need to ask someone to look after his heart. Gordon smiled his knowing smile, his small black eyes shining with a lifetime of knowledge and wisdom. "Hmm, well it is a great responsibility. Can you keep it safe and not let anything happen to it?" "Oh, yes!" cried Dilbert, becoming very excited at the prospect of being given this great honor. "You can count on me!"

Gordon considered it for a long moment, and then slowly nodded as he leaned back and rested his velvety paws on his ample belly. "Then I shall entrust it to you for one day," he said, "as a test. If you can care for it for one full day, you shall become an Official Keeper of the Heart." Dilbert could hardly contain himself. It was a wonderful chance to prove himself and he was determined to do a good job.

The next morning, Gordon reverently handed his heart to Dilbert and gave a solemn bow. "I trust you, Dilbert O'Sullivan, with my heart. Look after it well, for it is my most precious possession." After a deep breath, Dilbert gingerly took the heart with both hands and returned Gordon's bow with a somewhat clumsy one of his own. With that, Gordon made his way into Brian's suitcase and it was zipped up tight.

As he watched Brian depart, Dilbert became aware of how tightly he was clutching this valuable object and he felt a little shudder as the enormous responsibility finally sunk in. "What if I lose it?" he thought, feeling a panic rising within him. A voice Dilbert had never heard before stopped him in mid-thought. It was gentle and firm all at the same time. "Dilbert! Stop. You are kind and careful. You can do this." Who was that speaking? It was coming from inside his head. It was *his* voice, but not his voice. It was very strange, but it was so calming that he decided it could only be a good thing. Reclining on the sunlit window seat, he closed his amber-brown eyes and fell fast asleep.

Dilbert awoke from his nap and felt the sun warming his soft, silvery fur. He had a strange feeling that something wasn't quite right. He lifted his arms to yawn and have a good stretch and then—Gordon's heart! Where was it?! He frantically looked around in all directions, but it wasn't to be seen. It was gone! Oh, this was just awful. How would he ever break the news to Gordon? He imagined how upset Gordon would be, and what he might say. "Dilbert . . ." he heard faintly in Gordon's voice. Then it seemed a little louder and crisper. "Dilbert . . . wake up."

Dilbert opened his eyes and was more than a little surprised to find Gordon sitting next to him on a cushion with a big smile on his face. Confused, Dilbert looked down and saw the most glorious sight. Gordon's heart! He was clutching it so tightly, that it was bulging a little at the sides. "Wha . . . what happened?" muttered Dilbert, a bit bewildered. "I'm back from my trip," said Gordon in his rich, soothing voice. "You have been asleep for a very long time, you must have been dreaming." Dilbert, now a little more awake, was starting to feel extremely relieved. "You mean . . . I didn't lose your heart?" Gordon gave a little chuckle. "No, young Dilbert, you did not. You have done exceedingly well, and I hereby declare that you are an Official Keeper of the Heart."

With that, Gordon gently touched both of Dilbert's shoulders and then gave him a little wink. Dilbert had never felt so proud and his face beamed with delight. He gave Gordon a deep, respectful bow and delivered the heart back to its rightful owner.

"When I was scared," Dilbert said curiously, with a tilt of his head, "I heard a voice in my head. Who was that?" Gordon grinned and lifted his velvet paw in gesture. "Ah, that was your conscience." Seeing the overwhelmed look on Dilbert's face, he added with a loving smile "and that, young Dilbert, is a lesson for another day."

Notes

There are two character voices to create here. Remember that character voices in children's books are generally more fully developed. Young children want to be entertained above all else when they're being read to and learning to read themselves. To create the character voices, look for clues in the text about who they are and how they might sound:

Gordon is wise, patient, and knowledgeable. He is also a teacher and a guardian of Dilbert and comes across as the wise old sage or patriarch. The phrase from the text "*said Gordon in his rich, soothing voice*" is a gift which you won't always get and gives very clear direction as to how this character sounds.

Dilbert is the junior of the two. He comes across as sweet and naive and eager to learn and progress. These traits might translate into a lighter sounding voice with lots of enthusiasm and wide-eyed wonder. Keep in mind that the characters should have good separation as discussed in Chapter 4.

When you're narrating this script, be sure to animate your body and feel the joy of the story. You might also visualize reading to a young child to give the read more depth.

Performing Characters from the Inside Out by Dian Perry (Nonfiction)

As we discussed in earlier chapters, there is a vast difference between creating fully developed characters who are ready to be deployed, and the vocal gymnastics of creating a "silly voice." It is important to remember that characters for cartoons and video games must be as believable as any other type of character. Everything that an actor would put into creating a well-rounded character for stage or screen still applies—the only differences are that a) the voice is the only part of the performance to be captured and b) all physical movement must be silent.

In this chapter, we're going to look at the 4-step process for creating a character voice from an image:

Step 1—Image Brainstorm

Look at the character and write down everything you see. Don't delve into character traits or backstory at this stage— just note down what you see in the image (buck teeth, messy hair, huge blue eyes, etc.)

Step 2—Archetype and Backstory

Referring to the archetype list in Chapter 1, assign an archetype if you can, and create a backstory. If you have been provided with a character description, do not deviate from this but feel free to supplement it. Backstory elements could include age, name, family, hobbies, favorite food, and so on.

Step 3—Climb into the Character

Looking at the image, recreate the character's stance, making sure to take into account any facial expressions. Once that feels right, get moving as the character. When you're happy with that, allow a character voice to come through and blend that with the physicality.

Step 4—Character Notation

Make a note of all your choices, being as specific as you can so that you can recall the character later.

Notes

Most nonfiction audiobooks will naturally be a little more formal than their fictional counterparts. More often than not, you will be dealing with facts as opposed to story, but there are exceptions. For this particular nonfiction book, the performance can afford to be a little more lighthearted, due to the subject matter. This is a "how-to" guide for performers on character voice and your position is that of impartial narrator.

Audio Description (AD)

Most AD projects are recorded using specialized software, which combines the descriptions, video, and recording functions. The text to be recorded appears on screen with a preset duration and each block of recorded audio must fit within the time allotted. The writer will have determined the timings based on character dialog and how much of a scene needs to be described.

With this first set of descriptions, practice hitting the AD sweet spot—describing the scenes and action without being overpowering.

The Martian

Flying over the rocky, barren surface of the red planet toward sunlit rock formations in the distance. Debris from the previous night's storm lies on a sandy, rock-strewn slope.

A body in a spacesuit and helmet lies still, partially covered in reddish sand, and surrounded by scattered pieces of damaged equipment.

Watney jolts awake and gasps for air. He tries to roll over from his left side and realizes that he has been injured. His abdomen has been impaled by a silver, pencil-shaped piece of debris. He sits up slightly, wipes the sand off the instrument panel on his left wrist, and presses a button to cancel the alarm.

He raises himself to a kneeling position, plants his right foot on the surface, and pushes off his knee to stand. The piece of metal in his abdomen is attached by a wire to a satellite dish and snaps taught, bringing him back to his knees in pain. He removes a knife from his utility belt and cuts through the wire to release himself.

He stands and surveys his surroundings. The HAB is in the distance, but the Mars ascent vehicle is gone. He is completely alone on the planet. He slowly limps towards the HAB, holding his injured left side.

He approaches the camp and opens the outside hatch. Stepping through, he quickly closes it and moves the lever upward to the locked position. A cloud of artificial atmosphere is released into the chamber. He unlocks the inner hatch, walks through, and locks it as well.

He hurriedly removes his helmet and throws it to the floor. He frantically grabs the outer layer of his suit with both hands and removes it. He quickly unhooks his gloves and throws them down, unbuckles the bottom part of his suit, and removes his cap.

Looking down at the piece of metal stuck in his side, he steels himself and then yanks it out. He quickly removes the rest of his suit down to his waist, and is left wearing a tight, blue undershirt.

Grabbing a handful of surgical tools and holding his hand against his side, he cuts himself out of the undershirt, tears open a package of gauze with his teeth and presses it against the wound.

He carries the metal tray of surgical tools over to a desk, sits down in a chair and adjusts a mirror in order to see the wound clearly.

Notes

This set of descriptions covers only 3.5 minutes of the film. For long scenes such as this with no dialog, there will be much more information that needs to be conveyed to the viewer, which means denser descriptions and more of them.

The next AD project gives you an opportunity to practice with timings. Each description has a time limit. Practice each while timing yourself and see how you do. Some of the descriptions are tight, which happens a lot on AD jobs. The trick is to make the descriptions fit within the time, without having them sound overly rushed. If there is any time remaining, that's fine, as recorded descriptions are trimmed afterward.

When you're working on an AD project, you'll occasionally find that the timing for a description is simply too tight for what you need to do with the line. Sometimes, the writer doesn't take into account a pivotal emotional switch or the need for a pause if the scene changes mid-description. In these cases, it's fine to request an amendment to the text.

The Truman Show

A newspaper headline: "Crackdown on Homeless: Seahaven City Fathers say Enough is Enough!" Truman walks past the man holding the newspaper. He looks at the headline in disbelief, and then walks slowly through the square with a bemused look on his face. He enters the revolving door to his office building but instead of going in, he goes around twice and ends up outside again, looking even more confused (23 seconds).

A hidden camera pans back and forth, searching for its subject and once found, zooms in on Truman who has departed from his morning routine (8 seconds).

Truman continues to walk cautiously around the town square, eying everyone and everything suspiciously. He crosses the street as a city bus passes behind him and the hidden camera readjusts to center him in the frame (11.5 seconds).

Truman takes a seat on a curved stone bench next to a table with an umbrella. A bus passes in front of him and, once it's cleared, the hidden camera zooms in to find him again. Truman looks around thoughtfully at the bustle of activity in the square (13 seconds).

Audio Guide (Audio Tour)

Vintage Candy Museum

Welcome to the Vintage Candy Museum in Longmont Village—a truly magical place to revisit the sweetness of your childhood.

To begin your tour, press the green button on your handset. To stop the recording, press the red button; to rewind or fast forward in 10-second increments, press the back or forward arrows. You're all set! Our tour begins in the Great Hall of Candy. Step through the chocolate bar doors to experience the smells and tastes of your youth.

Directly to your left is a replica of the Little Candy Store, a famous Third Avenue landmark from the early 1950s until the late 1980s. Please watch your head as you step inside.

Children from the surrounding mountain neighborhoods would visit the store after school and on weekends for a striped paper bag of sweet treats. The variety of colors and choices was simply intoxicating. Sometimes, kids would spend half an hour or more, mouths watering, just looking and deciding how to spend the dollar their mother had given them.

All of the candy and novelty items you see in the wooden trays are real: red and black licorice whips, nougat, wax lips, chocolate in every shape and size, watermelon or apple bubblegum sticks, and hard candy in all colors and flavors. And who doesn't remember the giant, speckled jawbreaker and the classic candy necklace?

Although most are no longer widely manufactured, our specialist candy engineers (affectionately called "Loompas" in honor of Roald Dahl's beloved characters in *Charlie and the Chocolate Factory*) have painstakingly recreated each one. They are available for purchase in the gift shop at the end of your tour.

As you exit the Little Candy Store, to your left is our magnificent Taffy Island. This gigantic sculpture, with its palm trees, rocky beaches, turquoise water, foliage-covered hills, and wildflowers, is made entirely from saltwater taffy!

The artists, Bernie Loretta and Kenneth Virgil along with their team, spent approximately 1,100 hours stretching, chopping, melting, shaving, and sculpting over 500 pounds of the chewy candy to create this incredible work of art. All of the colors come from the taffy itself. Not a drop of paint was used anywhere. But they did use a whole lot of glue and resin, so please don't be tempted to take a bite!

As you continue around the Great Hall, you will arrive at The Nut Hut (please do not enter if you suffer from any type of nut allergy). This is where you'll find every kind of nut imaginable, covered in every kind of chocolate. From white chocolate pecan clusters to dark chocolate covered peanuts. Did you know that the peanut isn't really a nut? It's actually a legume! Feel free to try a sample or two from one of the golden trays.

The final stop on our tour of the Great Hall is the Cotton Candy Cloud. Standing 15 feet high and 20 feet in diameter, this huge multicolored cloud is made entirely of cotton candy! The 'rain' is made of translucent peppermint drops suspended on thin wires from the platform above and the lightning bolt is lemon curd, which has been dried, rolled out, and cut into shape. While the cloud looks good enough to eat, it was set with copious amounts of hairspray, so your cotton candy craving will have to wait until you arrive at the gift shop!

We hope you have enjoyed the Great Hall of Candy. Please step through the sour ball bead curtain for the next stage of your tour.

Notes

Your narration for this copy would be very informal (a rare setting of 1 on the formality scale) and lighthearted. After all, who would want to take a tour of a candy factory with a deadpan, serious voice in their ears? There should be lots of smile in this read and a very one-to-one, friendly delivery. The intention is to entertain, inform, and perhaps even tickle.

Remember that the visitor will have your voice in their ear throughout their tour of the museum. You are only addressing one person to enhance their experience, so your delivery should feel very personal and authentic.

Corporate Films

Capital Coaction

Leadership. Teamwork. Innovation. Without these core values and the top executives in the field, Capital Coaction would be just another financial products institution. But we are different. We have been creating the world's premier investment packaging product software for nearly 30 years and we are stronger than ever before.

Because of you, our dedicated team of professionals, the Synergistic Financial Platform is now the gold standard in the industry. SFP has consistently outperformed every direct competitor since its inception. But we're not stopping there.

We are bringing innovative products online every month. And with even more new ideas in the pipeline, we are set to disrupt the entire landscape of the industry.

We also view our global responsibilities through a lens of hope and charity. The Financial Freedom Initiative has already helped thousands of families free themselves of debt. And we have only just begun.

We are celebrating not only the past three decades of Capital Coaction excellence, but also our future prosperity. The launch of our Global Expansion Project has created a higher projected growth period than we had initially predicted and our entire team will share in this positive era together.

Capital Coaction—blending finance with heart for a brighter future.

Notes

Consider the highlighted portion of this sentence: "We have been creating the world's premier investment packaging product software for nearly 30 and we are stronger than ever before." It's easy to get lost during a read when you have a noun preceded by several adjectives, but you may recall the simple notation fix of square brackets from Chapter 4. If you use them around the entire phrase: [premier investment packaging product software] your eye will identify the word string as one item, so you won't be thrown by it.

In the second paragraph, you may have noticed the rather gnarly line: "since its inception last spring." That's a lot of "s" sounds and not the best choice of words to be spoken aloud (this happens more than you might think). Writers are sometimes so focused on the content, they don't always consider how it will sound when narrated. Depending on the circumstances, I might be inclined to ask for a script change here—perhaps "since it launched last spring."

Gladwell and Sons

We were there when your great-grandfather was getting ready for his first date with your great-grandmother. We were there when your grandmother soothed your sunburn after a day of making sandcastles on the beach. And we were there when your own babies were small and you wanted to keep their delicate skin clean and soft.

The world has changed since your great-grandparents were teenagers, and Gladwell and Sons has changed along with it. We are continually refining our signature products and creating new ones to not only enrich the lives of our customers but to help sustain the planet as well.

Gladwell and Sons are currently recruiting skilled chemists, who can help us develop our range of environmentally friendly products. It has never been more important for large corporations to get on board with responsible manufacturing and creating quality skincare products that don't cause harm to the planet.

For generations, our family's products have been part of your life and we are committed to being there when your great-grandchildren need us. We look forward to welcoming you into our family.

Notes

This is a straight-forward corporate read with a sentimental tone. For this type of narration text, you need to be careful that the emotion isn't false, forced, or overdone. If you allow yourself to really feel the message of this one and connect with it, the audience will connect with it too.

Documentaries

Sierra Chimp Sanctuary

Bobo is a recent arrival at the Sierra Chimp Sanctuary and is still apprehensive. He has not ventured outside his enclosure since he arrived six days ago, and the welfare team is eager for him to engage with the other members of his group. Now ten years old, Bobo was rescued from a private residence where he was severely neglected. He has not yet learned to trust that he is now safe and has a home for the rest of his life.

Lenora, who heads the welfare team, opens the gate to the paddock where the rest of the group is playing. She waits to see how Bobo and the other chimps will react to each other.

An hour has passed, and Bobo is still sitting in his enclosure, but he begins to watch the other young chimps through the glass with increasing curiosity. Victor, who arrived last year, is chasing George around the wooden play structure, while Leo and Nicki squabble over a fallen tree branch. Bobo slowly moves forward to get a closer look, but stops at the frame of the gate. Most of the other chimps show little interest in the new arrival.

Lenora keeps a close watch while one of the younger chimps slowly approaches. Lenny was brought to the sanctuary three years ago, after poachers killed his mother. He stops short of the enclosure gate and sits in a patch of long grass.

For the first time since his arrival, Bobo seems genuinely interested in another chimp. He takes his first few tentative steps outside his enclosure, and Lenny senses that it is safe to approach. He comes to sit next to Bobo and together, they watch the other chimps playing on the climbing frame. A new friendship is born.

Notes

The visuals for this piece would be live footage of the chimps and the members of the welfare team. This narration would not be wall-to-wall, but rather interjecting when additional information is needed. It's important not to upstage the visuals here.

Regarding positioning, the text doesn't indicate that the narrator would be a representative of the sanctuary, but it would be a good choice here.

The PATCO Strike of 1981

In August of 1981, President Ronald Reagan made a decision that would forever change the labor landscape in the United States—he summarily dismissed more than 11,000 federal employees.

Air traffic controllers across the country had dared to go on strike, citing unsafe working conditions, overall concerns for aircrew and passenger safety, and salary issues. The controllers paid a heavy price for their protest.

The year was 1968—the Vietnam War was still raging, Martin Luther King Jr. and Robert F. Kennedy were assassinated, and The Professional Air Traffic Controllers Organization (PATCO) was formed. Its initial purpose was to replace the Air Traffic Controllers Association (ATCA) which had been routinely failing to protect the rights of Federal Aviation Administration (FAA) controllers. In fact, the membership guidelines for the ATCA included a mandate that the majority of its directors should come from FAA management. Any controller concerns or complaints were directed to FAA and ATCA management and were oftentimes disregarded.

With the formation of PATCO, everything changed. Tracy Perry, a private pilot, flight instructor, and air traffic controller for over eighteen years, remembers what it was like in the early days.

Interview 1 VT

Unlike the ATCA, PATCO (later to become a labor union) specifically *excluded* anyone who worked in management. The new organization provided a much needed collective voice for its members to address any issues as professional air traffic controllers. But while PATCO's solidarity may have boosted morale, many member concerns still fell on deaf ears when management was approached.

The new contract between the controllers and the FAA was due to be negotiated in 1982. The issues on the table were clearly defined, ranging from unfairly calculated pay for overtime (required) to outdated radar equipment, and unsafe scheduling practices—which included a mandatory six-day work week and sometimes as little as eight hours between shifts. Most of these issues on their own could have serious consequences for safety, but there was even more going on behind the scenes. A great many controllers felt that the safety of the flying public was being jeopardized.

Dan ("Sky") Bishop explains.

Interview 2 VT

The fact that full-performance controllers were training new hires *while* working live air traffic was a great concern. As with flight training, an instructor needs to let a situation develop to an almost dangerous degree to test if the trainee is able to solve the problem. In addition, those who were tasked with training new air traffic controllers were not given any kind of classroom instruction on how to go about this. It was another valid concern which could have serious implications for safety.

On August 3, 1981, over 12,000 controllers walked off the job. President Ronald Reagan announced on national television that the striking controllers had three days to return to work or forfeit their jobs. There was no hearing or judicial action—simply an order by the president.

Many fired controllers submitted applications to the FAA. Management reportedly claimed that these controllers were "too old to do the work," a statement which contravened age discrimination legislation. This argument formed the basis of a lawsuit which was filed in Federal Court in 2005. At the time of filming, the case is still pending.

Notes

The visuals for this documentary would be archive footage and stills of air traffic controllers at work, the interviews with those who went on strike, and video of President Reagan at that time. The general intention might be to inform or educate, but a more refined one might be "convince" as the tone of the documentary seems to indicate that the strike action by the controllers was warranted. The pace would be on the slower side and would need to take its cue from the interviews. The documentary deals with an important historic event, so the tone would be quite formal.

E-learning

Junebug Guidance Services

Welcome to this e-learning for Junebug Guidance Services. In this module, you will learn the basics of the JB-1a platform which will include:

- Logging into the system with your secure passcodes and biometrics;
- Creating an individual or group assignment;
- Navigating Levels 1 and 2 of the Global Satellite System (GSS); and
- Transferring a task, project, or assignment to a Tier 3 project manager.

To begin, double click the blue JBGS winged logo in the task bar at the bottom left of your screen. A dialogue box will appear and you will be prompted to enter your login details. If you have not yet been assigned a secure passcode, you will need to contact the HR department and present your credentials before being cleared to access the platform.

Once you have entered your name, password, secure passcode, and ASC clearance code, you will be asked to use the scanner which was issued to you and calibrated specifically for you during your orientation and medical examination. Please note that your scanner must remain in the lockbox provided before and after each use and the key to the box must remain on your person at all times.

When the green light on the scanner stops flashing, you have been approved for entry. This may take up to 60 seconds. You will then see a white screen containing six blue boxes, which connect to the different subsections within the Universal Network. Access to each subsection requires a secondary passcode. Click the box marked 'New Mission' to highlight, then press Alt + N. Type in your specialist secondary passcode and press Shift + Z.

To create a new assignment, choose "New Assignment" from the left-hand drop-down menu, and then choose either "Individual" or "Group." Press Enter. The system will automatically assign a case number and a Tier 2 supervisor. Enter all of the assignment details, and specify the projected outcome. Press Alt + Y to confirm. Note: the system will not allow you to confirm the assignment unless all fields are completed. To return to the main screen, press and hold the Omega key.

This concludes Part 1 of this module. You will now be asked to answer a series of questions in order to check your learning. This will take approximately 10 minutes to complete. Click 'Next' when you are ready to begin.

Notes

E-learning generally calls for an intimate read with a one-to-one feel. The read for this copy would be quite formal due to the subject matter. Remember to keep the pace relatively slow to allow time for learning.

Strategies for Teachers in the Performing Arts

Welcome to this e-learning on Strategies for Teachers in the Performing Arts. This module will take approximately 30 minutes to complete. When you have finished, click "Next."

Active learning

Integrating active learning is vital for subjects in the performing arts. It would be unrealistic to expect students to develop performance skills solely by reading or listening to a lecture. Care must be taken while covering knowledge-based material to make lectures as brief as possible and to break up longer segments with student-centered activities.

Being mindful of active learning is most prudent during performance observation. Students not performing should be kept included and engaged. This can be achieved by discussing what is occurring and by encouraging them to support their fellow students and to give constructive feedback.

Learners vary greatly in terms of experience, age, and natural ability. It is important that each student is recognized and feels an integral part of the group and that those with more experience or natural ability not be given preferential treatment, nor be allowed to take over the class.

Initial assessment

Initial assessment (sometimes referred to as diagnostic assessment) for each student is necessary in order to establish a baseline for learning. Finding a starting point for learning content and skill level is important, but initial assessment is also useful for identifying other needs, such as functional skills or dyslexia, which may not have been previously disclosed.

A variety of assessment strategies can be used during the course, including oral and aural quizzes, performance and feedback, observational assignments, and worksheets to be completed during the session.

Performance and feedback is a valuable way to formatively assess learners in a performing arts environment. Post-performance, each student is first given an opportunity to assess and evaluate their work. This is followed by feedback from the other group members and then from the tutor. In this way, the student is receiving valuable information from several sources which they can then reconcile with their own observations and thus make a solid plan for improvement.

Motivation

Passion is infectious. A teacher who loves their subject and lets that enthusiasm show in the classroom will naturally create a buoyant atmosphere. This is a good start, but it does not mean that nothing more is required. The use of humor, real-world examples, and encouraging each learner to take part in discussions and feedback are just a few ways to engage and motivate learners. Please click the green button on the right side of your screen to watch a brief video.

Notes

This is a fairly straight-forward e-learning project and your role would be that of impartial narrator. The visuals (aside from the video introduced at the end) would likely be a slide presentation with bullet points. As there are no images for the student to take in during the module, the narration can afford to step forward a little, and be more of a driving force in the learning.

Explainer Video

Vitality Mixer

Congratulations! You are now the proud owner of a Vitality Mixer. In this brief video, we will cover initial assembly, operating procedures, and cleaning instructions to ensure that your Vitality Mixer lasts for many years to come.

To begin, ensure that all components have been included in your shipping box:

1 base unit with power cord and plug
1 plastic jug with integrated spinning blades
1 rubber lid with removable plastic cover
1 plastic tamping tool
1 rubber scooping tool
1 instruction manual
1 recipe booklet

Assembly

Putting together your Vitality Mixer is quick and easy: remove all packaging and recycle where possible. Wash the jug, lid, and plastic cover with warm soapy water, and dry thoroughly.

Place the base unit on a hard, flat surface and plug the cord into an outlet. Place the jug into the base unit, ensuring that it is firmly seated. You're all set!

Operation

To operate your Vitality Mixer, place the contents into the jug. Place the rubber lid onto the jug but leave the plastic cap off for now. Have the tamping tool ready.

Ensure that the middle dial is turned all the way around to the left (counterclockwise). Flip the switch on the right which will start the blades turning (caution: never insert anything into the jug other than the tamping tool). Using the middle control, slowly increase the speed (clockwise) until the dial is all the way around to the right. Once on its highest setting, flip the switch on the left. This is the highest speed for the Vitality Mixer. Use the tamping tool through the top of the lid to push down the contents of the jug while in operation.

Once the contents have reached the desired consistency, return both switches to the off position. Be sure to turn the dial all the way back to the left for next time. If the unit is switched on with the dial on the highest setting, you could end up with splashes of food on the ceiling!

Cleaning

To clean your Vitality Mixer, fill the jug to the halfway mark with hot water and add 3–4 drops of dish soap. Place the jug onto the base and run the mixer at full speed for three minutes. Rinse well and allow to air dry.

Notes

Your role would be as a member of the company. For some reason, many explainer videos such as this one tend to have an air of "sell" about them, which is odd as the customer has already made the purchase. The read should be upbeat, informative, and friendly.

Holiday Video Tour

Singer Hotel and Spa

The Singer Spa and Hotel in Berwang, Austria is your winter and summer paradise in the Tyrol. Enjoy an incredible day of skiing or snowboarding, then relax and unwind in the hotel bar or enjoy a treatment and a swim the world-class Singer Spa. The spa is located across the road from the hotel, accessed via a fully decorated underground passageway.

From the lower ground level of the hotel, open the door to another world. The tunnel is a perfect introduction to the relaxation which awaits you with the aroma of essential oils and soft music playing throughout. Once through the main doors to the spa, you can book a treatment, have lunch in the bistro, or relax by the indoor-outdoor pool and enjoy the stunning mountain views. On the lower level, you'll discover a different world with the herbal sauna, steam room, and waterbed room. Here, you are free to relax, listen to music, or have an afternoon nap to the sounds of the waterfall outside.

The nearest ski lift is open all year round, so you can enjoy a peaceful ride to the top of the mountain, even in the summertime. The only sounds you're likely to hear are the wind through the trees and the cow bells on the slopes below. The air is fresh and clean, and the views are nothing short of spectacular.

There are plenty of summer activities including mountain walks, guided hikes to the Zugspitze, and biking through the winding pathways in the village and beyond.

Once you visit the Singer Hotel and Spa in Berwang, you will want to come back year after year. We look forward to welcoming you soon!

Notes

Your intention for this type of script will be something akin to "enticing." The purpose of the voiceover and video is to tempt prospective customers to find out more or make a booking.

The visuals for this type of narration project will always be spectacular (anything not so wonderful wouldn't make the final cut of the video) so your narration will sit behind those images and either explain what is being seen or enhance it.

Grey Squirrel Ranch

Imagine yourself in a secluded forest getaway by a brook in the heart of the Rocky Mountains. This charming cabin sleeps six and comes complete with kitchen and indoor bathroom with shower.

This romantic hideaway is just over two miles off the main highway but when you're here, it will feel like two hundred. The only sounds you will hear are the wind in the pines and the surrounding wildlife. Whether you spend your days hiking, watching the hummingbirds, reading on the redwood deck, or feeding peanuts to the chipmunks, a week at Grey Squirrel is worth four at a seaside resort. It is the ideal remedy for the stresses of city life. But if you start to miss it, Estes Park is just a few minutes further up the mountain, where there is ample shopping, superb microbreweries, and restaurants for you to enjoy.

The scenery is breathtaking and the mountain air intoxicating. Treat yourself to a week at Grey Squirrel near Meeker Park and start creating wonderful memories for you and your family.

Notes

Your intention for this script would also be "to entice." The viewer will have the breathtaking images to look at, but will also need to feel the awe and wonder in the voiceover.

Interactive Voice Recording (IVR)

Elmer Publishing

Thank you for calling Elmer Publishing. If you know your party's extension, please enter it now.

For sales, press 1.
For marketing, press 2.
For accounts, press 3.
For opening hours, press 4.
To listen to these options again, press 0.

For all other departments, please remain on the line and an operator will be with you shortly.

Front Range Credit Union

Prompt 1

Thank you for calling Front Range Credit Union. Please note that calls may be recorded for training purposes and quality assurance. If you know the extension of the party you would like to reach, you may dial it at any time. You can access your account at any time using our Front Range Mobile App or by logging into online banking.

Prompt 2

Connecting you now.

Prompt 3

Sorry, that extension number is not valid. Please try again.

Prompt 4

Thank you for calling. If you know the extension of the person you want to reach, you may dial it now.

Prompt 5

Our offices are currently closed. Our contact center hours are Monday to Friday, 6am to 8pm and Saturday, 9am to 2pm Pacific Standard Time.

Prompt 6

Please listen carefully as our menu items have changed.

Press 1 to conduct a transaction using the Front Range Mobile App, our 24/7 automated account access system.

Prompt 7

If your credit card has been lost or stolen, please hang up and dial 1-800-555-7688.

Prompt 8

For more information about our products and services, please visit us at FrontRangeCreditUnion.org. To repeat this message, press the # key.

Notes

IVR is similar to on hold, in that it's one-to-one communication with a single person on the telephone. The main difference is that IVR is usually informational only (no sales) so the tone is more formal and matter-of-fact. The copy could be set out in any number of ways.

Language Training (LT)

Unit 11, Level 2—Let's Sing!

Activity 2

Whenever I begin to feel stressed or blue, I like to sing to make myself feel better. I put on my headphones, play my favorite music, and sing at the top of my voice. I am sure the neighbors wonder what is happening! If I know the song well, I will try to blend different melodies together. I can feel my mood change almost instantly. There are some songs I listen to when I want to feel uplifted and others when I want to feel calm. It just depends on my mood.

Sometimes, when I play a song that is very different from how I feel, I have to turn it off. It is too disturbing! For example, if I feel a little low, I cannot listen to very happy dance music because that is too big a jump in my mood. I have to choose something just a *little* happier than where I am and work my way up. What kind of songs do you like to listen to and sing along with?

Unit 2, Level 4—Fear

Activity 1

Host: Welcome back. We're talking today with my guest Dr. Elizabeth Hadley about fear. Dr. Hadley, can you tell our listeners more about the nature of fear and how we respond to it?

Dr. Hadley: Certainly. When we feel afraid, we enter a state which we call 'fight or flight'. The body prepares for one of two things: battling the object of our fear or running away. The example of the caveman and the saber-tooth tiger is often used and it's a good one. When he encountered this threat, his heart rate increased and his muscles prepared to either fight the tiger or run away fast. He usually did the latter.

Our bodies still respond to fear in this way, even though most of the time, we're not being chased by anything. The saber-tooth tiger is our own thoughts. There is external stress such as dealing with a trauma, working through conflict, or meeting a deadline, but then there is internal stress which comes from our negative thoughts and worries. Our body doesn't know the difference between real and imagined stress. It just gets ready to fight or flee. We can greatly reduce our stress levels by learning to quiet our minds and keep our breathing steady.

> *Host:* Thank you very much for being here, Dr. Hadley. This has been most illuminating. After the break, we'll be talking to a representative from the Mayor's office about the rising costs of road maintenance. Please stay with us.

Notes

One of the main things to keep in mind with LT is the pace. As with any type of learning material, the delivery needs to be on the slow side to allow the student to take in the information. But narration for LT is slower still, as the student is learning a new language. Just how much slower depends on the level of the course. Until you get used to it, narrating LT at the right pace for the project can feel excruciatingly slow, and you'll need to fight the impulse to speed up, which takes a lot of concentration. Diction is also very important and you'll need to enunciate much more than you would for other types of narration. There are generally no production visuals with LT projects. Students will, however, be following along in a workbook as they listen to the audio.

Medical

CAR-T Cell Therapy

Multiple myeloma (MM) is a hematopoietic malignancy which forms in the plasma cells of the bone marrow. It is generally accompanied by the development of osteolytic bone lesions. Treatments for MM include bone marrow transplants and proteasome inhibitors such as bortezomib and carfilzomib. As the disease is often recurring, more effective treatments need to be developed.

MM begins as a premalignant precursor condition called Monoclonal Gammopathy of Undetermined Significance (MGUS) then progresses to Smoldering MM (SMM) to active MM and eventually to end-stage Plasma Cell Leukemia (PCL).

B-cell maturation antigen (BCMA) is expressed on most MM cells. Protein receptors expressed on the tumor cell membrane during MM development are the ideal antigens for successful immunotherapies. BCMA is a member of the tumor necrosis factor receptor superfamily.

With chimeric antigen receptor T-cell therapy (CAR-T), T-cells are engineered to target a specific antigen on the surface of cancer cells and destroy them. CAR-T cell therapy has been shown to decrease malignant clonal plasma cells in Multiple Myeloma.[1]

Notes

There are some complicated phrases in this text and lots of pronunciation to clarify. Where possible, it's always best to research any medical terms yourself (rather than wait to receive them in the session), and there are useful websites that can help.

Medical narration is usually on the high end of the formality scale, but it does depend on who the audience is. For example, a medical video to reassure children about a procedure would have a very different feel to one aimed at top physicians.

Museum Display

The author and poet Kahlil Gibran was born on January 6, 1883 in Bsharri, Lebanon. He considered himself primarily a painter, but is best known for his written work, *The Prophet*, which was published in 1923.

The sea that calls all things unto her calls me, and I must embark.
For to stay, though the hours burn in the night, is to freeze and crystallize and be bound in a mould.
Fain would I take with me all that is here. But how shall I?
A voice cannot carry the tongue and the lips that gave it wings. Alone must it seek the ether.
And alone and without his nest shall the eagle fly across the sun.
Now when he reached the foot of the hill, he turned again towards the sea, and he saw his ship approaching the harbour, and upon her prow the mariners, the men of his own land.
And his soul cried out to them, and he said:
Sons of my ancient mother, you riders of the tides,
How often have you sailed in my dreams. And now you come in my awakening, which is my deeper dream.
Ready am I to go, and my eagerness with sails full set awaits the wind.
Only another breath will I breathe in this still air, only another loving look cast backward,
And then I shall stand among you, a seafarer among seafarers. And you, vast sea, sleepless mother,
Who alone are peace and freedom to the river and the stream,
Only another winding will this stream make, only another murmur in this glade,
And then shall I come to you, a boundless drop to a boundless ocean.[2]

Notes

This text forms part of a video display in a museum and the visuals would most likely be a mixture of images from the author's life and illustrations based on the text. For the introduction, the narrator's role would be that of outside authority; for the recitation, that of poet. During this latter portion of the script, the performance can afford to be very emotive and free.

On Hold Messaging

Manaugh Flowers

Thank you for calling Manaugh Flowers. All of our team members are currently creating stunning floral arrangements. Your call is important to us and someone will be with you shortly.

Do you have a special occasion coming up and need advice about arrangements or centerpieces? We have a huge selection, from the simple and elegant rose to the exotic bird of paradise. Ask one of our team members and they will be happy to guide you. Thank you for holding. We'll be with you as soon as possible.

Did you know that Manaugh Flowers does more than just flowers? We have a wide range of gift items, balloons, and party accessories, all available for next-day delivery. Ask one of our team members for more details. Thank you for holding. We appreciate your patience.

Manaugh Flowers is open Monday to Saturday from 7am to 7pm. You can also place an order on our website: www.ManaughFlowers.com. We have hundreds of arrangements to choose from and all are available for next-day delivery. Thank you for holding. Someone will be with you shortly.

Notes

When narrating on hold messages, you will always be speaking as a representative of the company. The communication is one-to-one, so it's personal and intimate. Given the subject matter of this particular script, the read would be very informal. Sincerity is also a key factor—no one likes an apology that isn't heartfelt, especially when they're being held captive on hold.

Point-of-Sale Video

Kitchen Cohort

Does this look familiar? You try and try to create evenly chopped vegetables, but can't quite manage to get to the end without fumbling or even injuring yourself!

With the new Kitchen Cohort, these problems will be a thing of the past. Peel, slice, dice, or chop: carrots, onions, peppers, celery, and even the tiniest cloves of garlic with this revolutionary kitchen utensil. It comes in a variety of colors, snaps apart for easy cleaning, and is completely dishwasher safe. You'll wonder why you ever settled for using an ordinary kitchen knife.

Make coleslaw in an instant, prepare vegetables in moments ready for a delicious stir fry, and chop your favorite fruit in seconds, ready for a healthy snack.

The Kitchen Cohort—available in the housewares section.

Notes

Point-of-sale videos ride a fine line between narration and commercials, so the "sell factor" is usually ramped up. This particular script would require a high-energy read, in order to attract the attention of nearby shoppers.

Satellite Navigation (Satnav)

Starting route guidance to your destination.
Continue to follow the road.
Continue to follow the road for ＿＿ yards.
Continue to follow the road for ＿＿ miles.
Turn right. Turn left. Take the next right turn. Take the next left turn.
Take the second right turn. Take the second left turn. Bear right. Bear left.
In one mile, keep to the right. In one mile, keep to the left.
In ＿＿ miles, keep to the right. In ＿＿ miles, keep to the left.
In one mile, bear right. In one mile, bear left.
In ＿＿ miles, bear right. In ＿＿ miles, bear left.
In ＿＿ yards, turn right. In ＿＿ yards, turn left.
In ＿＿ yards, make a U-turn.
…then take the next right …then take the next left.
…then take the second right. …then take the second left.
One, two, three, four, five, six, seven, eight, nine, ten, hundred
First, second, third, fourth, fifth, sixth, seventh, eighth, ninth, tenth
In ＿＿ miles…
In ＿＿ yards…
…take the ＿＿ exit.
Take the ＿＿ exit.
At the ＿＿ roundabout, take the ＿＿ exit.
Calculating new route.
Your new route has been calculated.
Your destination is ＿＿ yards on the right.
Your destination is ＿＿ yards on the left.
You have reached your destination.
Ending route guidance.

Notes

Satnav is one of the few areas of narration where attention to precision is warranted. For these projects, you aren't striving for a connection with the listener—just imparting directions and information (refer to the section on satnav projects in Chapter 3).

Where you see "..." in the script, that's an indication to read the line as a partial sentence. A trick for doing this well is to replace "..." with a possible line and say that in your head before (or after) reading the rest aloud. It's a bit like singing in a group—you may hum someone else's part in your head so that you can join in at the right time and at the correct pitch.

Where you see "_____," that's an indication to allow a space for a number. You'll need to pitch these sentences and the numbers in such a way, that they will edit together seamlessly.

For some automated systems (not necessarily satnav) you may also be required to read a sequence of words or numbers in three different intonations: beginning, middle, and end of sentence. This helps to create a more natural pattern of speech when the segments are combined. These projects require a very high level of focus and concentration, but can be very enjoyable once you get into a rhythm.

Technical

Tepla Aviation

Welcome to this information video on preflight procedures for the Cessna Model 152. This video is specifically for student pilots who are renting aircraft for instruction with a qualified instructor. In preparation for the preflight inspection of the aircraft, you must first check both the aircraft and aircraft engine logbooks. This is important in order to verify that all mandatory checks have been performed and logged so that the aircraft is legal to fly.

The preflight begins while *approaching* the aircraft. This is an excellent time to look over the aircraft, ensuring that all pieces are attached, there are no flat tires, no dings or dents on the metal, and that it appears to have been cared for.

Next, open the left door to the cockpit in order to make a cursory check of the interior. Place the keys on top of the instrument panel (this will become important later). Remove the gust lock on the control wheel so that the control surfaces have full travel: left, right, forward, and back. Turn the Master Electrical switch to the ON position. Check the level of fuel on the gauges and make a mental note of the fuel on board. Turn the Master Electrical to OFF. Behind the seat in the seat pocket, you will find a small plastic container with a probe sticking up through it. Take this with you, along with the dipstick for the fuel, and return outside.

Climb up the steps on the left side of the cowl with the long dipstick and check the fuel level in the tank. Note: never risk your life by assuming the gages are correct. Check that the level of the fuel is the same as the reading you got on the gauge for that tank. Ensure the cap is very secure when you have finished. Repeat this procedure on the right fuel tank. If you are in need of fuel, this is a good time to call the appropriate staff member to fuel your aircraft while you complete your walk-around.

Return to the left side near the cowling and in front of the strut to continue your inspection. On the side of the cowling is a very small hole that is the static air source. Your instructor can go into greater detail on the importance of this opening. Ensure that it is not covered with anything or it will not work properly.

Notes

Technical narration doesn't always mean that it's difficult to pronounce. It is a genre of voiceover where a project is created for a highly skilled audience. This particular project is for those who are learning to fly (a very elite group). The visuals could be animation, but are more likely to be live-action video of the aircraft and someone performing the preflight procedures.

Take this script slowly and take into account all the action which is going to be taking place on-screen. This is quite a formal piece of copy with very high stakes for safety. The tone for this text would be in line with a safety video in a commercial aircraft.

8 On the Job

We have now arrived at the business end of our work together. You've learned about authentic communication, the foundations of good narration, the different types of projects and how to approach them (and how not to), and you've practiced diligently until you are fully calibrated and in complete control of your skills. Now you have a booking.

This means that you'll either be recording with your own equipment (if you have it) or you'll be traveling to a studio, where you'll be greeted by a client (or three) and a generous helping of adrenaline. You did great work when you were on your own, but now you have people in the room watching you and that can change things. Holding on to your authentic core and turning in a solid and connected performance just got a little tougher.

You need to remember that you weren't just plucked off the street at random—you were invited. You either auditioned for the job or were cast based on your narration reel and/or an agent singing your praises. You've already established that you belong in the room—now you just have to deliver the goods.

The Studio

Studios can be intimidating places; it doesn't even matter if they're plush and luxurious or very basic. When you arrive at reception and announce that you're there to do a voiceover, your heart will probably beat a little faster. This is perfectly natural. After all, the whole reason for you being there is to bring the client's project to fruition; to put the finishing touches on their creative "baby," which may have been weeks or even months in the making. You're bound to feel a little pressure.

When you walk into the studio, the first thing to do (after politely greeting everyone with a smile and a firm handshake), is read the room. It's likely that the rest of the team will already be assembled and hard at work when you arrive. It may be that they have all worked together before and know each other well. You'll need to sense the atmosphere and conduct yourself accordingly. If you don't, it can make for an awkward start. For example, if you burst onto the scene with a bouncy, keen-to-please energy, and everyone else is in a somber mood, this could be a little irritating for them. My advice is to go in pleasant, slightly upbeat, but otherwise neutral. You can then get the lay of the land and take it from there.

If you're already feeling self-assured and capable, that's terrific. But if you're a little shaky, try to stay centered until you get comfortable. Don't pretend that you feel super confident—that will only make matters worse—just be polite, listen, and stay alert. When you get settled into the booth, you'll probably begin to feel comfortable and more like yourself.

Like anything, confidence comes from doing. After you've delivered the goods a few times and seen the relieved faces when your performance blends seamlessly with the rest of their project, your confidence will grow and you'll look forward to rising to each new challenge.

The Client

The vast majority of my clients are lovely; we get along well and produce great work together. They're generally happy to recommend me to others, and I'm happy to recommend them to voiceover colleagues as good clients. We do this not only because we trust each other's work but because we can vouch for the other's integrity.

It's important to make a human connection with those you work with. If you see each other as real people who are trying to do their respective jobs well, your collaboration will be more enjoyable and the quality of your work will be much higher. You don't necessarily have to invite your clients to your wedding; just take a genuine interest in who they are as people.

Artistic Differences

Unfortunately, it doesn't always go so smoothly and sometimes, you and your client simply won't be on the same page (figuratively speaking). Picture the scene: you're in a session, you have thoroughly prepped, set your foundations, and now you're delivering a read which you feel is solid, connected, and ticks all the boxes. You're in full flow, fizzing with the feeling of the message, and . . . they're just not buying it.

When this happens, take a deep breath and stay calm. You don't yet know why it's not working for them, but it's your job to find out and then fix it, if you can. Be open and receptive to their feedback and make it clear that you're committed to delivering the read they're after. Keep in mind that the issue may have nothing whatsoever to do with you. For instance, the client might have had a specific syntax or melody in their head and when your read didn't match, it was jarring for them. Perhaps they're having a bad day, or maybe they're just looking to flex their director muscles.

I once had a difficult session where the client was listening remotely. He made it very clear that he hated the read I was giving. His manner was abrupt (to put it mildly) and it was quite challenging to remain calm. I encouraged him to clarify what he needed so that I could translate it into "narrator speak"—intention, formality, emotional set-point, and so on. He was having none of it and proceeded straight to the last resort of the desperate director—the dreaded "line reading." If you haven't had the pleasure, it's when someone reads you a portion of the script as they imagine it should be read.

Some voice actors don't mind them, but few things during a session make my heart sink faster than being given a line reading, especially when it's accompanied by the phrase "I'm not a voice actor, but you get the idea." We're then forced to rapidly ascend from the depths of our carefully crafted performance to the sandy shallows of "Imitate this, please, but make it sound good." This can leave us with a painful case of the bends.

Back in the session, I knew I would have to switch things up and deliver the read mechanically (rather than intuitively) until the client was satisfied. I had to completely change my approach and try to view the performance through his eyes. It wasn't easy, but we got there in the end.

For us artistic types, it can be heartbreaking to abandon our own creative process in favor of someone else's, but there will be occasions when you'll just have to. Sometimes, your beautiful oil painting will be interrupted and you'll have to settle for painting by numbers to get the job done. Remember, you're providing the brushes, colors, and technique, but you don't own the finished artwork.

The Session

Every client session is different, whether you travel to a studio, or work online. The best advice I can give you is to be prepared, relaxed, open, attentive, and amenable. The rest you can figure out as you go along.

Keep in mind that many clients don't get to work with voice actors all that often and find it kind of a thrill. I've turned up to high-stakes sessions expecting it to be very stressful, only to discover that the five clients in the studio were almost in a party mood. They'd been let out of the office for a few hours to do creative work with a voice actor and they were loving it.

Reset after Each Take

The more takes you do in a session, the easier it becomes to lose sight of your foundations. What happens is that you essentially start imitating yourself from the previous take, so the read becomes more superficial each time. Always do a quick internal "reset" before each take—reconnecting with who you're talking to and why.

Your Two Cents

I've always found one of the trickiest things to navigate during a voiceover session is sensing when it's acceptable to make suggestions. Even though everyone is ultimately on the same team, there's still certain etiquette to be followed. You're a latecomer to this creative task force, so it's not a good idea to storm the barricades on your high horse, spouting all kinds of suggestions and ideas on how their project could be improved.

Respect is the order of the day. Your colleagues have put a lot of effort into this project and knocking the script into its current shape (whatever that may be). You have no idea how many previous versions have been rejected or why. It might be that the script change you're about to suggest was already tabled weeks ago and shot down by the end client. Let the session develop a little before putting in your two cents, and then do so with finesse.

For example, if you come across an issue with sentence structure, read it as written, then gently suggest that it might flow better if x, y, z, were moved around. Ask the client if they would like an alternate take (alt). Unless the script has had to pass through many corporate gates for approval, they will usually appreciate the input.

If there's a simple typo in the copy or an obvious grammatical error, it's usually fine to make the change without comment. Everyone who is following along with the script will know that you've done this and be silently grateful.

So, here's what I've learned about making suggestions in a session: everyone present can tell when the text isn't easily rolling off the tongue and are usually grateful for ideas which will improve it, but choose your battles wisely—too many suggestions can be perceived more like scolding than collaboration.

The Party's Over

When everyone is happy with the narration read that you've delivered, your role in the voiceover session is over. Even if you've all had a good laugh together and you're feeling a real sense of camaraderie, it's time for you to go. There is final production work to be done which doesn't involve you. So, unless you've been invited to stay, thank everyone involved, say your goodbyes, and exit gracefully.

The Solo Session

Recording a narration project in isolation is a very different undertaking than working with others in an outside studio. Your experience will depend on elements that are unique to you—personality, work ethic, and what type of environment you need to create in order to do your best work. I can't speak to what it will be like for you, but I can provide some insights about what I've learned from my own experience of working solo, how it differs from working with others, and the challenges it can bring.

Whenever I'm working in a studio with people watching, I am focused. I come alive when there's an audience—it gets me revved up and my creative juices flowing. I enjoy the real-time exchange of ideas and knowing instantly when the client has what they need from the performance.

Working solo is another matter. I only have myself, the script, and the microphone. It's much easier to get distracted, so I really have to raise my level of awareness and discipline. This is where understanding my own narration machinery is critical. For example:

1. If I start making silly mistakes, there is probably some kind of mental clutter to be cleared.

2. If I stop for no good reason, that's usually an indication that I've slipped into looping syndrome and started to monitor myself.

3. If I wander from focused expression to controlling the read, that's my perfectionist tendencies coming to the surface.

It's been an interesting learning curve over the years, discovering the quirks of my own personal narration system. Of course, the fix is always a variation on a theme: recenter, refocus, revisit the foundations, and re-engage physically and emotionally.

In summary, I wouldn't say that I prefer recording on my own to working with others in a studio, but there are many things I enjoy about it. For instance, I can go at my own pace, take a break whenever I need to (and for as long as I need to) and I'm free to talk to myself without causing anyone to worry about my mental health. By the way, if you do feel the need to talk to yourself during a session, please let it be encouraging and kind.

The Demo

It wasn't part of the original plan to include information about narration demos in this book. I was determined that the primary focus would be the "psychology" of the craft—how to manage MBV in order to communicate authentically and deliver great performances. I also wanted the work to be universal, without highlighting any differences between nations or regions regarding rates and other business practices. But then I realized that it simply wouldn't be fair to take you through everything you need to know to be a great narrator, and then leave you high and dry about the primary tool that you'll need in order to find the work in the first place.

The following questions are nearly always asked during workshops and coaching sessions and I've tried to provide guidance that would be relevant to all, regardless of geographic location. I suggest that you always do your research on current trends and specific requirements for your area before investing in a demo.

How long should my narration demo be?

I suggest two minutes maximum. Narration demos can afford to be a little longer than other voiceover demos, as you'll need to demonstrate your ability to deliver and sustain a longer read.

You may be tempted to make your reel longer to show absolutely everything you can do. Please don't. Put yourself in the producer's shoes—they simply don't have the time to sit through a five-minute demo. Some would even balk at listening for two, but if you wow them in the first minute, they'll be more likely to listen to the second.

What material should I include?

There isn't a one-size-fits-all answer to this question. It depends on what kind of work you want to pursue and what type of projects suit your voice. If there is an area of narration you don't think you would enjoy, there's no point including a sample, and then crossing your fingers that nobody books you for it. Include examples of work that you *want* to do and that you would be right for. Refer to the projects list in Chapter 3 for ideas.

How many clips should there be?

I suggest between four and six clips as a guide, but it obviously depends on how long the clips are. If you're a good all-rounder, you may be tempted to include more samples and make them shorter. I would advise against this. Include your strongest reads which show your skills and range. Don't worry about including every type of narration genre under the sun. A producer who is casting for a satnav project won't pass you by just because there's no sample of one on your demo.

How long should each clip be?

A good guide is between fifteen and twenty seconds, but leave yourself flexibility. The length of each clip depends on what you're trying to demonstrate with it. For example, an audiobook clip could be a bit longer as you'll need to highlight various skills: storytelling, the ability to portray different characters, and switching between the narrator and character voices. Incidentally, if you're very keen on narrating audiobooks, I suggest creating a special demo just for them. Show an array of genres and styles that you're interested in narrating.

I have recording facilities—can't I just produce the demo myself?

Even if you have a home studio, I strongly suggest that you *do not* produce your own demo *unless* you are a demo producer yourself or a trained sound designer/engineer.

Good demo producers keep in touch with current trends and know what potential clients are listening for. They may even be able to help you get your copy together and advise on the best order for the clips. Most importantly, demo producers can make you sound great and are a valuable second set of ears. Entrust the production of your precious demo to a professional. Apart from skills, it is your most important tool as a voice actor.

How do I find a good demo producer?

There are so many demo producers across the globe and it can take a while to find a good one who is the right fit for you. My advice is simply to do your homework—ask around for recommendations and search online. Then get in touch to ask about their experience and the services they offer. Visit their website and listen to samples of their work. The packages offered vary greatly, so always find out what's included in the price—how many hours of recording, any pre-production assistance, help with scriptwriting, and how many changes they allow after the demo is edited.

Recording your first demo can seem daunting, so find a producer you feel comfortable with—someone who will be honest with you and gently guide you through the process.

Should there be music or sound effects on the demo?

If appropriate for the clip, then yes. For example, music and sound effects would form a natural part of a documentary sample but not an audiobook. You want your demo to be comprised of samples that sound like excerpts from real projects.

There are different opinions within the industry about whether clips should be taken from actual work or specially created for the demo. Here's where I stand: you have more control over the finished product if everything is written and produced from scratch. The production values will be consistent, and you will also be free to showcase whatever you want, without being limited by work you've actually booked and happen to have a copy of.

While researching demo producers, if you come across a sample of their work that consists of a series of clips with one long music bed underneath, move on. The illusion of real work has been broken. Part of the job of your demo is to sweep the client away in the story you are telling, the information you are imparting, or the product you are describing. As soon as their attention turns to the production values or the construction of the demo itself, you've lost them.

Words of Wisdom and Final Thoughts

A surprising portion of this book was written on my phone while sitting on various trains, planes, and buses. Concepts and content would pop into my head; I would take out my phone, write it all down, and then transfer it to the main manuscript later. It took me a while to figure out what made the writing flow so well when I was in transit. The answers eventually distilled into these four little nuggets of voiceover wisdom:

#1 Relax

I would be sitting on the train, relaxed with my eyes closed, mind free to wander, then *bam!*—ideas for the book started pouring in. Because I was still, my "conduit" was available for an inspirational download and all I had to do was take dictation.

In a voiceover session, when you're feeling tense and uptight, you're essentially putting a knot in the works and making it tough for inspiration to squeeze through. The more calm and open you are, the more intuitive and connected your performance will be.

#2 Lower the Stakes

While on the train, I wasn't in "book-writing mode," with all the internal pressures and mental noise that can bring. I was simply jotting down a few ideas while I was on my way to go do something else.

When you're booked for a narration project, of course you'll want to do a good job, but nobody is going to die if you make a mistake. None of the other team members are perfect humans (guaranteed) and, contrary to how you might be feeling, none of them expect you to be perfect either. Hold on to the truth that they're just people, trying to do their jobs well like you are.

#3 Slow Down

I happen to be a really fast typist, so when I'm writing at my desk, my fingers move faster than the thoughts and words coming to me, which can make me feel a little impatient. Writing on my phone is much slower (I use the index finger method as opposed to flying thumbs) so it creates more space for the ideas and words to stream in.

When you're in a voiceover session, slow yourself down. Go easy on the sugar and caffeine, unless you have a high tolerance. You will nearly always have some adrenaline surging, so refer back to tips one and two, take a few deep breaths, and enjoy every moment you have at the microphone.

#4 Surrender

I have my husband to thank for this one. He pointed out the lack of control while on public transport. Someone else was always in the driver's seat, so I didn't have to think about it. Also, there was little else I could be doing, so distractions were kept to a bare minimum.

In voiceover, trust that you've set solid foundations, thoroughly prepped all aspects of the job, and then just surrender to the message you're conveying.

Safeguard Your Integrity

In your career as a voice actor, I can almost guarantee that you will at some point be offered work that doesn't fully align with your values or ethics. You may desperately need the income, but think carefully about accepting work that you'd rather no one hear. Recordings are forever, so be discerning about which projects you want your voice and your name to be associated with.

Many years ago, I was offered an audiobook by a new client who categorized the project as "chick lit." I'd not heard the term before and just assumed that it would be a romance novel. I agreed to do the job and signed a contract. Then the book arrived.

I started to read and within a dozen pages or so, I realized that this particular "chick lit" title was closer to pornography. Now, I'm a fairly open-minded lady, but I blushed my way through the first read and started my prep, while seriously wondering how I could get out of doing this job.

In the end, I refused to be the voice actor who breaks a contract, so I bit the bullet and spent a very squirmy week recording something I would never want my father to hear. Since then, I've been much more careful about what I sign on for and have kept my vow to never again breach my integrity for a paycheck.

Final Thoughts

This book was written during tumultuous times. Brexit, presidential impeachments, natural disasters, economic uncertainty, civil unrest, and a global pandemic were all vying for my attention while I explored subjects of a more subtle and introspective nature. It wasn't an easy time, but it was certainly a lesson in remaining centered against a backdrop of chaos (I was not always successful).

During the writing process, it occurred to me that guidance about developing and improving narration skills could also be applied to our own lives:

1. Managing personal energy and the quality of the vibrations we send out into the world.
2. Creating without analyzing.
3. Internally clarifying our intention when we speak.
4. Communicating authentically.
5. Allowing honest emotion to infuse our language.
6. Cultivating awareness.
7. Recognizing when we're off track and setting a course correction.

Perhaps the timing of this book was no accident. We seem to have entered a period of intense transformation on so many levels, which is both exhilarating and unsettling. Now more than ever, we need honest communication and connection.

I like to think that through refining how we deliver our clients' messages and stories, we'll become better able to express our own, and perhaps bring a little more light into the world.

Appendix

Narration Toolbox

Throughout this book, I've shared various tools, lists, and worksheets to help you prepare and perform different types of narration projects. They've been gathered together here (in the order in which they were introduced) for easy reference.

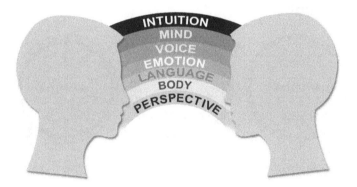

Figure 1 The 7 Wavelengths of Communication.

Foundations of Narration

Mind–Body–Voice (MBV)

The primary system of voiceover performance. The components must be balanced and work together in harmony.

Positioning (point of view)

Usually indicated by the text.

Corporate—company representative or outside authority?

Audiobook—impartial narrator or character in the story?

Who am I and who am I talking to?

Who are you as the narrator and who is your audience?

Visuals

Narration supports and supplements what is being seen.

The 3 Dials

Figure 2 The 3 Dials.

Intention—What are you trying to do with this communication?

Pace—Based on subject matter, emotion, and timings.

Formality—Depends on the audience.

Emotion

What is the overriding emotion of the piece?

List of Intentions

advise	enthrall	placate
amuse	enthuse	prepare
announce	entice	present
assist	escort	persuade
attract	establish	prime
awaken	excite	prompt
beguile	explain	propose
brief	fascinate	provoke
cajole	galvanize	reassure
captivate	guide	recommend
caution	illuminate	remind
charm	incite	revive
coach	induce	reward
comfort	influence	school
commend	inform	seduce
convince	instigate	sell
counsel	inspire	shock
dazzle	instruct	soothe
delight	intrigue	stimulate
demonstrate	introduce	stir
denounce	invigorate	suggest
describe	invite	teach
document	lament	tell
educate	launch	tempt
elucidate	mesmerize	tickle
enchant	motivate	train
encourage	move	unite
endorse	mystify	urge
energize	nominate	update
enlighten	notify	usher
entertain	pacify	warn

Narrator Archetypes

The Manager (gold standard)—Key to maintaining: Balance

The Analyzer—Key to overcoming: Trust

The Worrier—Key to overcoming: Confidence

The Perfectionist—Key to overcoming: Letting go

The Monitor—Key to overcoming: Focus

The Bulldozer—Key to overcoming: Patience

The Anticipator—Key to overcoming: Presence

Foundations Worksheet

Who am I? Who am I talking to?	
Positioning What is my role as the narrator?	Company representative Outside authority Other_____
The 3 Dials: *Intention*: (refer to the List of Intentions) *Pace*: 1–10 (1 = very slow) *Formality*: 1–10 (1= very informal)	 1 2 3 4 5 6 7 8 9 10 1 2 3 4 5 6 7 8 9 10
Visuals: What else could I visualize in order to enhance the read?	Film, animation, stills, screen capture Other_____
Notes on emotional set-point:	
Notes on gesturing:	
Any other performance notes:	

Notation

1. "/" divides a compound sentence into separate thoughts.
2. ( ) marks a less important phrase. When you're in the middle of a read, parentheses help you see in a split second that everything within them is a side note and you'll know instinctively how to deliver it. It's also a good way to break up overwritten sentences.
3. [ ] groups word strings. When you're immersed in a complex read, your eyes recognize very quickly that everything within the square brackets is essentially one thing, which keeps you from getting lost in awkward sentences.

Yvonne Morley's (abbreviated) Vocal Warm-Up:

Physical preparation (tension release):

1. Shoulders (rolls, shrugs).
2. Neck (hang your head, move in half-circles between your shoulders).
3. Jaw (relax open and say "yah yah yah" and repeat as needed).

Breath preparation (abdominal release):

1. Breathe all the way out on a long "SHHH" (your tummy should firm/tighten).
2. Relax and breathe in again (your tummy should soften/ expand slightly).

Vocal preparation (vocal range and resonance):

1. Lip trilling up and down your range.
2. Gently hum to feel vibration (with a hand) in upper chest, throat, nose, and face.

Speech preparation (articulation):

1. "Big chewing" to move lips, cheeks, nose, chin, and eyebrows.

Audiobook Foundations Worksheet

Fiction or nonfiction?	
Genre (science fiction, romance, historical, etc)	

Positioning

What is my role as the storyteller?	Impartial narrator
	Character within the story
	Other_____
What can be said about the potential audience? (sci-fi fans, history buffs, romantics, students, etc)	
How will this knowledge affect the style and feel of my read?	

Intention

(refer to the List of Intentions)

Additional Notes

Notes

Introduction

1 Rollin McCraty, Ph.D., *Science of the Heart, Exploring the Role of the Heart in Human Performance (Vol. 2)* HeartMath Institute, 2015, 36–7.

Chapter 1

1 Bruce Lipton, Ph.D., "We Communicate Through Energy," UPLIFT, March 30, 2017, www.youtube.com/watch?v=Zy-vkYQz12Q, accessed April 4, 2020.

2 John Hagelin, Ph.D., "How Vibration Affects our Body," www.youtube.com/watch?v=EQxDAaXuyvs&list=WL&index=66&t=3s, accessed June 18, 2020.

3 Rollin McCraty, Ph.D., "*Connecting with the Heart's Intelligence,*" SAND, March 28, 2019, www.youtube.com/watch?v=KurPSsFNZK0&list=WL&index=10&t=2s, accessed April 4, 2020.

4 David Bressan, "Nikola Tesla's Earthquake Machine," *Forbes*, January 7, 2020, www.forbes.com/sites/davidbressan/2020/01/07/nikola-teslas-earthquake-machine/#43a3b7f952c5, accessed September 28, 2020.

5 Hagelin, "How Vibration Affects our Body."

6 "How Hearing Works," www.hearinghealthfoundation.org/how-hearing-works, accessed September 29, 2020.

7   www.merriam-webster.com/dictionary/voice, accessed
    September 28, 2020.

8   Nina Kraus, Ph.D., "Feel the Vibrations: Understanding the
    Hearing-Emotion Connection," *The Hearing Journal*, Volume 70,
    Issue 9, September 2017, 52–3, www.journals.lww.com/thehe
    aringjournal/FullText/2017/09000/Feel_the_Vibrations__Unde
    rstanding_the.14.aspx, accessed September 9, 2020. Used with
    permission.

9   www.merriam-webster.com/dictionary/resonate, accessed
    September 28, 2020.

10 Fanny Gribenski, "Plenty of Pitches," Nature Physics, Volume 16,
    February 6, 2020, 232, www.nature.com/articles/s41567-019-
    0707-1, accessed September 28, 2020.

11 Anthony Holland, "Shattering Cancer with Resonant Frequencies,"
    TEDx Skidmore College, December 22, 2013, www.youtube.com/
    watch?v=1w0_kazbb_U, accessed September 28, 2020.

12 Sara Childre, "Raising Our Vibration Through Compassion and
    Unconditional Love," HeartMath Institute, April 4, 2017,
    www.heartmath.org/articles-of-the-heart/raising-vibration-
    compassion-unconditional-love/, accessed September 28, 2020.

13 www.merriam-webster.com/dictionary/flow, accessed May 10,
    2020.

14 Mihaly Csikszentmihalyi, "Go with the Flow," Wired, September 1,
    1996, www.wired.com/1996/09/czik/, accessed May 10, 2020.

15 McCraty, *Science of the Heart, Exploring the Role of the Heart in
    Human Performance (Vol 2)*, 24.

16 Gregg Braden, "How to Harmonize Heart and Brain," www.youtube.
    com/watch?v=237WCALmJXQ&list=WL&index=14&t=190s,
    accessed April 4, 2020.

17 Rollin McCraty, Ph.D., "Heart-Brain Coherence," Quantum
    University, November 6, 2018, www.youtube.com/watch?v=M
    O3SGkI3B-I&list=WL&index=9&t=1963s, accessed April 4, 2020.

18 Braden, "How to Harmonize Heart and Brain."

19 www.collinsdictionary.com/dictionary/english/intuition,
    accessed September 28, 2020.

Chapter 2

1 Jill Bolte Taylor, Ph.D., "My Stroke of Insight," TED Talk, 2008, www.youtube.com/watch?v=UyyjU8fzEYU, accessed September 28, 2020.

2 Patrick Fraley, www.PatFraley.com. Used with permission.

3 David Eagleman, *Incognito: The Secret Lives of the Brain* (Random House, 2011), 22–23.

Chapter 4

1 Ann Marie Chiasson, M.D., M.P.H. (Andrew Weil, M.D.), www.drweil.com/videos-features/videos/heart-center-meditation/, accessed September 17, 2020.

2 Yvonne Morley, www.yourvoicebox.co.uk/, App: Voice Coach. Used with permission.

Chapter 5

1 Maya Angelou, *I Know Why the Caged Bird Sings* (Random House, 1969), 106.

2 www.merriam-webster.com/dictionary/calibrate, accessed September 28, 2020.

3 David Hanscom, M.D., "The Connection between Anxiety, Anger, and Adrenaline," *Psychology Today*, December 15, 2019, www.psychologytoday.com/gb/blog/anxiety-another-name-pain/201912/the-connection-between-anxiety-anger-and-adrenaline, accessed September 28, 2020.

4 Lynne McTaggart and Bryan Hubbard, "Take a Deep Breath," What Doctors Don't Tell You, July 26, 2020, www.scribd.com/article/470606844/Take-A-Deep-Breath, accessed September 28, 2020.

5. Roderik J. S. Gerritsen and Guido P. H. Band. "Breath of Life: The Respiratory Vagal Stimulation Model of Contemplative Activity" Frontiers in Human Neuroscience, October 9, 2018, www.frontiersin.org/articles/10.3389/fnhum.2018.00397/full, accessed December 30, 2020.

Chapter 7

1   Yu-Tzu Tai and Kenneth C. Anderson, "Targeting B-cell Maturation Antigen in Multiple Myeloma," Immunotherapy, November 2015, 7[11], 1187–1199, www.ncbi.nlm.nih.gov/pmc/articles/PMC497 6846/, accessed April 13, 2020; "Bortezomib (Velcade)," Cancer Research UK article, www.cancerresearchuk.org/about-cancer/cancer-in-general/treatment/cancer-drugs/drugs/bortezomib, accessed April 13, 2020; "Car T cells: Engineering Patients' Immune Cells to Treat their Cancers," National Cancer Institute article, July 30, 2019, www.cancer.gov/about-cancer/treatment/research/car-t-cells, accessed April 13, 2020.

This text is for narration practice only. It does not necessarily reflect the current state of cancer treatment, nor is it intended as medical advice.

2   Kahlil Gibran, *The Prophet*, Penguin Classics; Illustrated Edition, January 15, 2019, 2–3.

Index